C000069288

We Get There by Walking

Paul Alcorn

Parson's Porch Books

www.parsonsporchbooks.com

We Get There by Walking
ISBN: Softcover 978-1-949888-68-3
Copyright © 2019 by Paul Alcorn

All rights reserved. No part of this book may be reproduced or transmitted in any form or by any means, electronic or mechanical, including photocopying, recording, or by any information storage and retrieval system, without permission in writing from the publisher.

We Get There by Walking

Contents

Sermons

Reflections

Prayers

Introduction

The fall after I graduated from college, I spent a month living at a contemplative retreat center in high desert outside of Sedona, Arizona. Silence was the order of the day…and of the night. Those who lived or stayed at the center spoke only at meals or to give instructions for the daily work we did to maintain the center, and during our morning and evening worship services. The rest of our time was spent in silence.

In the entrance to the retreat center's common space hung a banner with these words: *Pilgrim, there is no way. You make it by walking.*

As my time at the center was ending, I took a small piece of paper, sketched a person walking and added the words from the banner. I folded the piece of paper up and put it in my wallet.

That scrap of paper is long gone, but the words have stayed with me. *Pilgrim, there is no way. You make it by walking.*

Now, more than ever, I understand the truth of those words. All you or I can do…

The best you and I can do…

Is to walk in the direction of our best dreams and our bravest hopes.

To walk in the direction of promises of God which are meant for us and for all. And, that is what I am trying to do.

I invite you to walk with me.

Sermons

Neighbors

It was either the famous Swiss theologian, Karl Barth or the renowned preacher, Harry Emerson Fosdick for whom John D. Rockefeller built the Riverside Church in NYC, or maybe both who said: *"The responsibility of a preacher is to step into the pulpit with the Bible in one hand and the newspaper in the other."* That being true. This story.

As many of you know, I grew up in a small community just outside Pittsburgh, PA. The great, great grandchild of Scottish immigrants who, along with so many of their countrymen and women, made their way from Scotland to Ireland to either to western Pennsylvania to work in the steel mills that lined the Allegheny and the Monongahela Rivers or to Kentucky and southwest Virginia to work in the coal mines of Appalachia. Like all those other waves of immigrants before and after them, among the things they brought with them to their new homes was their religious traditions which, for these Scotch Irish immigrants was Protestant and primarily Presbyterian which is why I am who I am. One example of how this played out in my life is that, even after several generations, as a boy growing up, I was not allowed to wear green on St. Patrick's Day because green was the color worn by Irish Catholics. Irish Protestants wore orange.

I share that with you because if you were to ask me, when I was growing up, who my neighbor was I would have told you to look around me. Everyone I knew was white. Most everyone I knew was Protestant, and probably Presbyterian. I only knew two Roman Catholic families even though there were others in our community. And, St. Scholastica, the Roman Catholic Church in our neighborhood, had a hedge around it taller than I was. I remember walking past the church, looking through the opening for the gate and wondering what was back there behind all those hedges. I had no idea. Growing up I did not know anyone who was Jewish or Muslim or black or Latino. Everyone I knew looked like me.

All that began to change for me when I went to college.

The country was at the tail end of the civil rights movement and in the middle of the anti-Vietnam War movement. The college I attended had a black fraternity and international students. I was aware of them and knew some of them, but none were in my circle of close friends. That is context for this. The summer before my Junior year in college, after failing as a door-to-door salesman for Fuller Brush (Remember them? And, yes. I really did that.), I found a job working for Youth Opportunities Unlimited. A summer day camp program in the part of the Pittsburgh that went up in flames when the news hit that Martin Luther King, Jr. had been assassinated.

I can't remember how I heard of the program or how I got the job, but there I was. One of a handful of white youth in a community that was nearly 100% black working for an organization focused on providing a safe summer program for African-American children and youth. It was the first time in my life I was the one with the different colored skin. That summer challenged me in many ways and made my world a bit larger and more complicated as I grappled with the question *"Who is my neighbor?"*

After graduating from college, I found a job in a state-run institution for what we now call those who are developmentally disabled. Then they were called mentally retarded. It was the first time in my life I had been around anyone with that level of disability. I worked on a locked ward with 16 profoundly retarded adults all of whom were bigger and stronger than I was. It was the hardest and most inhumane job I have ever had. Those 16-24 months put me in touch two very different types of individuals. One was those who were seriously trying to make a positive difference in the way our communities and country understood and handled individuals with disabilities. The other were those who were dismissive and often abusive of those who were different and disabled. My world, once again, became a bit larger and a bit more complicated.

A couple years after Shodie and I were married and living in suburban Chicago, a friend stopped by to visit us. For several summers, we had been camp counselors together at a Presbyterian Church camp. As we talked and caught up with each other, he told Shodie and me he was gay. It was the first time someone I knew came out to me. A year or so later a different person made an appointment to see me. He came

14

by my office and asked me to pray over him in order to cast out Satan. He had been taught and told it was Satan who was making him gay. Several years later, when we had just moved to Bedford, a child of the church ask if her relationship to another woman could be acknowledged and blessed. This was before Holy Unions and marriage equality were even on the horizon. When her request became public a number of people left the church and, because I supported her request and said so publically, some walked out the door telling me I was not a Christian and did not deserve to be a minister. And, the question hung in the air for all of us to answer. *Who is my neighbor?*

Then there were the work trips to Appalachia and to Nicaragua with high school students to repair homes or to build homes. And, the conversations with those young adults about how it is possible that there are people in our country who live in homes with no indoor plumbing or in homes with roofs that are caving in or floors that have rotted away. Or, when we were standing in the dirt front yard of Rufina Amaya, the sole survivor of the El Mazote massacre. Do you remember ever hearing about that? Salvadoran troops had received training at the School of the Americas in Georgia, were flown back to El Salvador and then immediately flown to El Mazote where they rounded up everyone in the village, several hundred men, women and children, and massacred them as a message and threat to other communities in an effort to keep them from supporting the rebels who were fighting the dictatorial Salvadoran government. Rufina stumbled and fell as she and others were being rounded up. She lay hidden and listened as her husband and children and neighbors were shot. Standing in that dirt front yard with us, she talked about what had happened and about the challenge of forgiveness. In a way I had never done before, I grappled with the question *"Who is my neighbor and how large a circle am I willing to draw around my life?"*

I share all that with you because somewhere along the way I also began to take the Bible seriously and to take God seriously and to take Jesus seriously. Not so much as a list of things I am to believe or a creed I am required to say, but as a choice I make about the type of person I want to be and the values around which I wanted to build my life. The seeds for all that were planted by those who were members of the Aspinwall United Presbyterian Church. That all white, very traditional,

15

mostly conservative congregation. And, yet it was in that community of faith that I was encouraged to learn and to memorize Bible verses that somehow stuck with me. Lodged not just in my memory, but also in my heart and soul.

Treat others as you would like to be treated. Lord, when did we see you hungry?

Whatever you do for one of the least of these.

What does the Lord require of you but to do justice, to love kindness and to walk humbly with God?

Search me, O God, and know my heart. Test me and know my thoughts. See if there is any wicked way in me.

Blessed are the peacemakers.

And, this…

The parable of the Good Samaritan which we heard read a few moments ago. The lawyer standing up and asking Jesus what he must do to inherit eternal life. The question was not what he needed to do to get into heaven. But about what must one do to live a deep and full and meaningful and purposeful life. The answer given by the lawyer and affirmed by Jesus is clear and was understood by both of them. Two sentences from the heart of Hebrew scripture, one from Deuteronomy and the other from Leviticus, which were understood to sum up the entire Torah and all the writings of the prophets.

Love God.

Love your neighbor as yourself.

Then the real question. The hard question.

The question which I think is the most critical and most important religious question of the day. Not just for Christians, but also for Jews and Muslims and Buddhists and all others. A question I regularly ask high school students as we grapple with the intractable poverty which plagues places like Appalachia or complex geopolitical politics of places like El Salvador or Nicaragua.

Who is my neighbor?

And, how large a circle do we draw around our lives? And, how do we understand compassion and mercy.

I know there are political responses to this question. And there are economic responses to this question. And there are sociological responses to this question. But here you and I are...

In a church.

Immersed in and surrounded by a Christian liturgy and tradition. Celebrating World Communion Sunday.

And, from that context the question lingers waiting for our response. This is where I will leave it.

With that question.

Is the definition of *neighbor* the people of my childhood? Those who looked like me and went to church with me? Who had the same background and history as me?

Or is my neighbor those who are black and who lived on the North Side of Pittsburgh or who, in our own community, are sometimes followed around when they walk into a store? Or what about those who are gay or transgender whose desperation leads them to ask me to exorcise the demon from them or worse yet, in despair, take their own lives? Or what about those who are Jewish or Muslim as attacks, both physical and verbal, on them are on the rise? Or those who are mired in poverty in one of wealthiest countries in the world? Or those who have suffered under decades of dictatorships, many of which were supported by our own government, and who long for opportunity and a chance? Whose skin is brown? Whose primary language is Spanish?

As you plunge the depths of your own faith and allow the witness of the Bible to rattle around inside your heart, mind and soul. And as you look at the community in which you live and the circle you draw around your life, how will you respond to the question asked of Jesus and the story he told?

I believe how we answer the question makes all the difference in the world.

Signposts: And, It Was Good

Let me begin this morning with a couple of assumptions.

You may or may not agree with them, but at least you will know where I am coming from.

1. Being a Christian involves more than being a member of a church or showing up for worship on a Sunday morning.

2. As a Christian, how you act on Monday is at least as important, if not more important, than the prayers you recite and the hymns you sing on Sunday.

3. Following Jesus is not easy. The words may be easy:

Love God. Love neighbor. Treat others the way you would like to be treated. You are the light of the world.

But, living those words each day, every day is hard work and involves trying and falling short and trying again. It involves patience and persistence and practice and prayer.

4. There is no one way to be a Christian or a person of faith or to believe in God.

While religion and religious practices provide a helpful framework, the truths we each figure it out as we go. You make your way by walking.

Maybe I should just stop there and let all that sink in a bit or allow some time for questions or comments or even debate, but there is a bit more I would like to share with you this morning.

So, here we go.

Some of you may remember, from this past fall, my idea for periodic reflections about signposts or markers that help us find our way on our journey of faith. I came up with the idea this past summer while I was hiking on the Long Trail in Vermont, a trail which runs from the Vermont/Massachusetts border to the Vermont/Canadian border.

Right now, I am a few miles shy of being halfway done. The trail is marked by 2 inches by 3 inches white marks on trees usually located a couple hundred yards apart. While most of the time the trail is obvious there are times when it is only those white blazes on the trees that confirm you are still on the path. As you can imagine, hiking 8-10 hours a day provides ample time to think. While hiking, this past summer I realized faith, at least my journey of faith, is more like a hike in the woods with more roots and rocks and up and down than it is a walk in the park. If that is true then what, I wondered, are the markers we should be looking for to help us find our way and to not get lost. So, this morning is the second in a very sporadic series of reflections about signposts and markers. And the marker I would like to suggest this morning are these four words found in the opening pages of the Bible: *And it was good.*

The Biblical affirmation is that:
Creation is fundamentally good.
People are fundamentally good.
You are fundamentally good.
I am fundamentally good.
Those with whom we agree are fundamentally good.
Those with whom we disagree are fundamentally good.
Now before you get too far, with your all your *buts*…
But what about this?
But what about that?
But what about him?
But what about her?

Let me say that this statement is first and foremost a statement of faith more than it is a statement of fact. In the affirmation it makes, it asks the fundamental question about what direction you will face and about the vantage point from which you will view your life and the lives of others and the world in which we live.

Here is a bit of background about this passage from the Bible.

Despite popular perceptions to the contrary, this passage is not primarily about creation.

The core message is not about God creating the world in six days and resting on the seventh. And, it is not written as a *pie in the sky, Pollyanna, everything is nice and sweet and will be okay if you just trust God* point of view. It was, in fact, written at a time of deep political and spiritual crisis for the Jewish people. Then it was inserted as the Prologue to Hebrew Scripture; the starting point from which you should read and understand the rest of the story.

Here is the backstory to Genesis 1:

The Jewish people believed they were God's chosen people. That God had made a special covenant/a special promise with them. And there were tangible signs that confirmed that covenant:

The Ark of the Covenant which held the tablets of the 10 Commandments.
The Promised Land.
The land they believed God had given to them.
The city of Jerusalem.
The Temple in the Jerusalem.
And, a God appointed king to lead them.

Yet, here they were in exile.

All they had believed in and believed to be true had been destroyed.
They had been conquered by the Babylonian Empire.
The ark and the commandment tablets were lost.
Jerusalem and the Temple were destroyed.
The king was dead.
They no longer lived in or on the Promised Land.

When all seemed lost and life was at its worst, the very real question they asked was this: *Had God abandoned them?*

Out of that time of chaos and crisis of faith when all they had believed in was now lost and gone came these four words: *And it was good.*

And, here is where these words and this witness can become signposts for our lives.

Recall that time when your best laid plans fell apart. That time when even though you had done your best and done everything right life came crashing down around you. That time when you walked through what the Psalmist names as *the valley of the shadow of death*.

The diagnosis was grim.

A job was lost.

A loved one died.

You have been there. I have been there. We all have been there.

And, in that moment we are left to decide.

Will we become bitter and resentful?

Will we turn away or turn inward and let life dry up within us? Or, will we find another way?

I am not talking about platitudes like *when life gives you a lemon make lemonade*. I am talking about something more fundamental than that.

Something more important than that.

Something more difficult than that.

I am talking about the choice we make in those darkest moments... To choose goodness over hate.

To choose goodness over resentment.

To choose goodness over despair.

To choose goodness over bitterness.

To choose goodness over hopelessness.

I don't know how to tell you to do that.

There is not some magical step-by-step approach.

All I think I know is that the wisdom of the ages points us in that direction. That there is something about faith…

Something about the best of who we are and can be…

Something about what we know and name as God…

That bids us turn and face in that direction.

So, as we stumble our way forward on that journey, we call faith allow me to suggest four words from the Bible around which we might orient our lives which, in turn, might help you find our way:

And it was good.

Before You Go

A Sermon for the Sunday on Which We Recognize Graduating High School Seniors

Four years ago, when you were in Confirmation, there were probably one or two times when I said to you: *"I want to make sure that, at least once, you have heard a pastor say this…"* Whether that was about ways to read and understand the Bible or about sexual orientation and being inclusive or about my understanding of and relationship to those whose faith tradition is different than ours. Today, I want to that again. Before you go off to college and step towards that new tomorrow, given the public perception of Christianity and faith/religion, in general, I would like to remind you of this. To make sure, at least one more time, you have heard a pastor who takes God and Jesus and faith seriously say this.

First, God is…

Maybe it is easier to begin with what I think God is not.

Several years ago, I attended a national gathering of church leaders. One of the buttons being handed out read: *God Is Not a Boy's Name.* The message of the button was primarily about the patriarchy which is still prevalent in both church and culture, but it also serves as a reminder that, even though *he* is the pronoun used far too often, God is not male. Or female. Or up in the sky. And, God is not Christian. Or Jewish. Or Muslim. Or…you fill in the blank.

So, if that is not God, what or who is God for me?

I can respond to that question in several ways, but for this morning let me remind you of what I probably said to you four years ago in Confirmation. What if we thought of God as more of a verb than a noun? More as an action than a person. What if God is the source, the inspiration, to be found in acts of:

Compassion. Kindness. Justice. Forgiveness. Peacemaking. Gratitude.

In those moments when you do those things or experience those things or see those things, there is God.

Here are places I see and experience God.

I experience something of God when the Cherub Choir sings. I see God when meals and conversation are taken to someone who is sick. I stand in God's presence when we stand in front of a house we have helped to build in Nicaragua and the family talks about their 16'x16' home as their mansion and the gratitude they feel. I am surrounded by God when I leave my phone at home and walk in the woods or look up at the night sky. God is present when I and we work with others to make our congregation and our community and our country and our world a bit better today than it was yesterday.

In all those times and places God is. Where is God for you?
I hope you take the time to notice.

Second, how large a circle and which way will you face?

Religion or faith or God...whatever word you would like to use...is about the circle around your life and about which direction you will face. Some people use their faith to make the circle around their life as small and as tight as possible in order to define who is in and who is out and who is right and who is wrong. Do it my way or our way and you are in. Don't and you are out. Believe this way and you are in. If you don't you are out. Look like me. Talk like me. Dress like me and you are in. If you are different you are out. I think, often, that way of thinking about God or faith or religion is harmful and does violence to others. And, those who define God that way look like a football huddle. Facing inward. Only looking at each other. Backs turned to the world.

My understanding of the witness of the Bible and the teachings of Jesus is that we are to make the circle around our lives not smaller, but larger. Not only inviting people in but moving it outward until it encircles more and more.

The witness of the Bible is that all are made in the image of God.
All of us are named as children of God.
And we are called to be neighbors to each other.
And rather than facing inward and walking backward, we are to face outward; to see and to recognize those in front of us for who they are.
And to walk forward until they are encircled.

Third, know the story.
I have never read the Bible cover to cover.
I have tried, but I have gotten bogged down in genealogies and lists and laws. And, I am not asking you to. But, I am encouraging you to know enough of the story that when those moments of decision or judgement or choice come up in your life you have a touchstone and a point of reference which will help you decide what to do or how to act or which can be a source of understanding and strength.

That story...
Our story...
Includes what I read this morning.
Blessed are the merciful.
Blessed are the peacemakers.
You are the light of the world.
Treat others as you would like to be treated.

And, what about the stories in the Bible about confronting giants, because there continue to be giants in our world. Or, what about the stories of not wanting to do what you know you are supposed to do or called to do? For those moments will arise in your life. And, what about the stories of sowing seeds of making a difference or being blind and then being able to see. Know *those* stories.

And, notice I said *story* and not Bible.
That is intentional.
Again, going back to Confirmation. I urge you to read the Bible as story and poetry and not as science or a newspaper. The Bible is inspired and contains truth, but it is not meant to be read literally.

Fourth, community.

Look around you.
You probably know some of the people here.
You probably recognize a few others.
But there are many here you probably don't know.
That is okay.
But here is the thing.
All these people are the ones who, in ways large and small, have cared for you and prayed for you and supported you. These are the people your parents chose to stack around your life to help you grow up to who you are today.

As a community, we are far from perfect, but we try.

We try to care for one another.

We try to support one another. We try to challenge one another.

We add our faith and our hope and our money and our energy to the community called Bedford Presbyterian Church in order to do what we can to make the world closer to what we think God intends.

The question I have for you is this.

As you step towards what comes next in your life, what is that community going to be for you? The community which will support you and encourage you and challenge you to do and be your best?

Where are you going to find it? What is it going to look like?

What values do you want it to hold out in front of you?

What I think I know is it will look different than this. Different from what I have known and from what you have known growing up here. What I hope is you is this:

That you have the vision and the courage to find it and shape it and to be a part of it. That it does for you tomorrow what this community has done for you as you grew up.

And finally…

The comedian, Jimmy Fallon, was the surprise guest speak at the graduation ceremony at Marjory Stoneman Douglas High School in Parkland, FL. Do you recognize the name of the school? It is where, on Valentine's Day, a fellow student killed 14 classmates and 3 staff members. Taking that that tragedy and pain, a number of those students launched the #NeverAgain movement and, this summer, will be traveling the country registering young adults and encouraging them to vote. I read Jimmy Fallon's speech and would share this part of it with you because it applies to each of you, as well.

Most commencement speakers, they'll get up here and talk in the future tense. 'You will succeed. You will make us proud. And you will change the world. Most commencement speakers say, 'You are the future.' But I'm not gonna say that, because you're not the future. You're the present. You are succeeding. You are making us proud. You are changing the world, so keep changing the world and keep making us proud.

Don't Fit In

A Sermon for Confirmation Sunday

I am certain you already know this, but just to make sure. I speak for Kathy as well as myself when I say that when she and I talk with you about what it means to follow Jesus or about how we think about and imagine God, it is more than just words and more than just what we are supposed to say or do. In all the conversations we had over the last year, we were sharing with you something that is an important part of our lives. Something she and I take seriously and, even though, like you, she and I still have a lot to learn, our faith is something we do our best to put into practice each day. For us God is not a man in the sky. Or a woman, for that matter. Or a person with a beard. Or a person period. A force, maybe. A presence, yes. At least for me. I can tell you there have been times in my life when I felt there was something more with me or around me or holding me up or pushing me forward.

But most of the time, for me, my faith in God and following Jesus is a choice I make. A choice about the type of person I want to be and about how I want to live and about how I want the world to be and not about believing a certain list of things or feeling a certain way or making it to heaven someday. Getting to knowing you from our Sunday conversations and reading through your Statements of Faith, I think you get that.

So, here is what I want to say to you today starting with a snapshot of the world in which you live.

From the hallways of your schools to the seats of power and probably everywhere in between there are people who put other people down.

Who think it is okay to make jokes about those who are different? Or, exclude those who don't quite fit in.

All to make themselves look better or feel superior or maintain their place in the pecking order. And, racism is real and racist incidents are on the rise.

As are attacks, both physical and verbal, on Jews. On Muslims. On immigrants. On those who don't have what you and I have. And, there are some people use religion like a wedge.

Or, a hammer. Or even as a weapon.

My way or no way. My way of thinking or believing or acting or you are wrong or bad or going to hell. So, get out of the way.

And, all that is only a start.

I find all that hard to understand when I believe all of us…each and every one of us…is a child of God. Made in God's image.

I find all that hard to reconcile with the Bible when it says God is love. And, with what I know about Jesus who included those whom others did their best to ignore or to turn away or to exclude.

So, I am going to ask you to do something and to be something I am not sure I was able to do or be when I was 14 or 15. But, I am going to ask anyway.

And, that is don't fit in.
Dare to be different.
Dare to think differently.
Dare to believe differently.
Dare to act differently.
Take what we have talked about this year and what you wrote about in your Statements of Faith and transform those words into actions. Make them a part of who you are and how you try to live each day.

And, don't just be kind. Be courageously kind.
Even if it means standing up or speaking out.

Don't just be nice young men.
Treat others…all others…with respect.
Treat others…all others…the way you would like to be treated if you were in their shoes.

Take what you know about God

Take what you understand about what it means to follow Jesus and live it.

Lead the way.

Whether about gun violence or inclusion or the environment. Or, about racism or sexism or how you answer the question "Who is my neighbor?"

Do that.

Then, push me and others to follow.

Please.

Now What?

Last week, after a full and wonderful Easter Sunday morning, I went home and took a nap. After sleeping for an hour or so, I woke up to the realization that another Sunday was just around the corner. A Sunday which, with all my focus on Holy Week and on being ready for Easter, I had not given a moment's thought to. So, on Monday morning scrambling to catch up, I put my boots on and made my way to the church through the snow. At my desk I flipped through my file folder of notes and scraps of paper looking for some spark of inspiration. Something which connected with the Sunday after Easter and which both caught my attention and tugged at my heart which is the only way I know to write and preach sermons.

What I found was this.
Scribbled sometime in the past on a scrap of paper.
Loaves and fishes. Not much. What the little boy had.
That note sent me flipping through my Bible to find the story. You can also find the story in Matthew, but John's Gospel tells the story this way.

After this Jesus went to the other side of the Sea of Galilee, also called the Sea of Tiberias. A large crowd kept following him, because they saw the signs that he was doing for the sick. Jesus went up the mountain and sat down there with his disciples. Now the Passover, the festival of the Jews, was near. When he looked up and saw a large crowd coming toward him, Jesus said to Philip, "Where are we to buy bread for these people to eat?" He said this to test him, for he himself knew what he was going to do. Philip answered him, "Six months' wages would not buy enough bread for each of them to get a little." One of his disciples, Andrew, Simon Peter's brother, said to him, "There is a boy here who has five barley loaves and two fish. But what are they among so many people?" Jesus said, "Make the people sit down." Now there was a great deal of grass in the place; so they sat down, about five thousand in all. Then Jesus took the loaves, and when he had given thanks, he distributed them to those who were seated; so also the fish, as much as they wanted. When they were satisfied, he told his disciples, "Gather up the fragments left over, so that nothing may be lost." So they gathered them up, and from the fragments of the five barley loaves, left by those who had eaten, they filled twelve baskets. When the people saw the sign that he had done, they began to say, "This is indeed the prophet who is to come into the world."

Most of the time when we hear or read this story the focus is on Jesus and the size of the crowd and how there was not just enough food, but when all was said and done there was food left over. And, we are left to think about and marvel at how that all happened. But my scribbled note was not about the size of the crowd or about Jesus or about how it might have happened. My note was about the little boy and his five loaves of bread and his two fish. I don't know whether, for him, that was a lot of food or not much. Was the five loaves and two fish enough to feed his family for the day or for several days or for the week? But it is what he had. And, what he had, he shared.

I can imagine the situation. And, the naivete.

Most of us who have had children or been around young children have probably experienced something similar. Adults wrestling with an adult sized problem. A child over hearing what was being discussed and offering to help with what she has.

Her toy.

Her quarter.

Sharing her sandwich.

Sweet, but so insignificant when compared to the need or to the challenge at hand.

Except here. In this story.
Here, two fish and five loaves...
What the little boy had and offered...
In a crowd of 5000 men, women, children, grandfathers and grandmothers, uncles, aunts and cousins...

Here, two fish and five loaves were enough.

I think this story and that scribbled note on a scrap of paper I found in my file folder resonates with me today because I am weary. I am weary from the winter and the snow. I am weary from the effort and energy of getting ready for Easter and Easter Sunday. I am weary from losing my Mom a couple months ago and from worrying about

Shodie's Dad. I am weary from watching the news. And the current state of our country and the dysfunction of our politics. I am weary from hearing about another shooting. And, our polarized shouting matches which keeps us from taking steps to address the issue. I am weary of our President bullying people and calling them names.

I am weary because I believe the world should be different.
And our communities different.
And our neighborhoods different.
And our schools different.
And our families different.
And, I am weary because I believe I am to be a part of helping to make them different.
Making them better.
Making them just a bit closer to what I think God intends.
Making them safer so children don't have to be afraid in school or black families don't have to have *the conversation* with their sons, which I never had to have with mine, about how they are to act when approached by the police.

I am weary. And right now, I feel I don't have much to bring to the table. How about you?

So, is it grace?
Or, hope?
Or, reminder?
Or, encouragement?
Or, promise?
Or call?
That two fish and five loaves of bread are not only enough, but more than enough.

Roll Back the Stone

A Sermon for Easter Sunday

Easter.

And, April Fool's Day. Hmmm.

Where should I start? Let's try this. Knock. Knock.

[Who's there?] Jesus. Wait. Wait. Or not Jesus?

Enough! I think I should stop right there.

But my intuition tells me that somewhere in this complicated, startling, life and world turned right side up story is some sort of divine joke and God is laughing at the wonder of it all.

So, on this Easter/April Fools Sunday, I add my welcome as we gather this morning to celebrate Easter...beyond bunnies and baskets and decorated eggs.

As I read and reread and thought about what I wanted or needed to share with you this morning about Easter and about the message and meaning of the resurrection, I found my attention and imagination pulled in two different directions. The first was this. The realization that instead of this being one story – whether you read the resurrection narratives as something which happened to Jesus or something which happened to the disciples – the accounts of the resurrection, in fact, tell two competing stories. And you and I are left to decide which story will be normative for our lives.

The first story is one we know all too well.
It is a story about power wielded by violence and intimidation and fear.
All in the name of peace.
Rome with its legions of soldiers.
And, the roads of the Empire lined with crosses used for executions.
And, the Emperor named and treated as a god.
With those who had having more than what they needed.
And, those who did not, never having enough.

This story is not unique to the Bible.

It is the story of Empire which has been reenacted countless times in human history. The Assyrian Empire. The Babylonian Empire. The Roman Empire. The Inquisition. Nazi Germany. Syria today. The Philippines today. Jim Crow. Segregation. The Ku Klux Klan. The Alt-Right.

We know it. We live in it.

Its headlines fill the news.

Even today.

Again today.

Then there is this story.

The story of Jesus.

Who healed those who were broken?

Who fed those who were hungry?

Who welcomed those who were forgotten and pushed to the edges?

Who challenged the power and the story of the religious and political elite?

Who lived the reality that the circle which encompassed God's children is larger? As a colleague said, *"Moving the margins until there are no more margins."*

He said things like…

Blessed are the peacemakers.

Do not judge.

Treat others as you would like to be treated.

Be compassionate as God is compassionate.

Love your enemies. Do good to those who hate you.

Blessed are those who are gentle, but strong. They shall inherit the earth.

And, as crazy as all that sounds given the world as it was and is some people actually believed him. And began living that way.

Two stories.

On one side is the cross and the power of the Empire.

On the other side is the stone rolled away and the tomb that is empty.

On one side is the finality of death.

On the other side is the women meeting Jesus in that cemetery and disciples running for their lives meeting him on the road to Emmaus.

One side are the guards sent to protect the tomb falling over like dead men.
On the other side is Jesus who was dead experienced as being present and alive again.

And, like countless others before us, we are left to decide.
Which of these two stories will you use to shape the narrative of your life?

Let me ask that again.
Which of these two stories will you use to shape the narrative of your life?

And, my second pondering about the Easter story is this.
What came first?
Jesus' resurrection?
Or, the stone being rolled away?
I think we often assume the resurrection came first.
Jesus ready or already gone when that entombing stone is miraculously pushed back. But, what if that not the case. What if Jesus remained dead until that stone was removed? If that is true, then what about today? I ask because I believe if the Bible contains any truth at all, it is never just about then, but also about now. And never just about them, but also about you and me.

So, back to the question.

What if Jesus remained dead until that stone was rolled back?

Then what does that say about today in all those places where Death still reigns? And, violence still rules. And, fear wraps itself around their lives strangling life until it is no more?

In Aleppo?
In Parkland?
In Paris?
In Sacramento?
In Sandy Hook?
In New York City?

Next door?
Any and all places where Jesus is still dead?
If so, who will roll away the stone?

So, here we are… Easter 2018.

My prayer today for all of you…

For all of us…

Is this.

May whatever stones still entomb be rolled away that new life might emerge. And may the promises of Easter turn your world and our world right side up.

Are You Ready?

A Sermon for Christmas Eve

So here we are. Almost Christmas.

Most of us have spent the last several weeks getting ready. Trees bought and decorated.

Gifts bought and wrapped. Holiday parties.

Family gatherings. Cookies left out for Santa.

Cards and letters sent far and wide. All wonderful.

And here we are. In this place.

Together with family and friends and neighbors. Which is as it should be.

Together we sing the familiar carols. We light and hold our candles.

We retell that age-old story.

Silent Night. Holy Night.
Wondrous star led thy light.
With the angels let us sing.

All beautiful.

Take it in.

But here's the thing.
For all our preparation and for all the beauty around us I can't help but wonder if there is something more. Something we miss in all our other planning and preparation. All our decorations and gift giving. So much of what we spend time and energy and money on seems to have little to do with that simple, provocative, age old story we read together each year.

A story so familiar we almost know it by heart.

Gentle Mary. Stoic Joseph.

Shepherds in the field abiding. Angels from the realms of glory.

A story so layered over by tradition and Christmas card images and soften by the glow of candles that the meaning and the challenge the story presents gets lost in the pageantry of our celebration. You know the story, but maybe you miss the tension. Here it is.

Caesar Augustus. Roman Emperor. Self-proclaimed Son of God on one side.

Jesus. Born in Bethlehem. Laid in a manger. Gospel proclaimed Son of God on the other side.

King Herod in his palace and on his throne in Jerusalem.

Or, Mary and Joseph making their way from Nazareth to Bethlehem.

The Roman legions who patrol countryside and streets to impose their peace.

Or, the heavenly hosts with their proclamation of *Peace on Earth. God's good will to all.*

As we hear the story, we are left to ask ourselves and then to decide.

What is this story really trying to say?

Which side of the story will we chose as our own to guide and direct our living? And, because the Bible is never just about then, but also about now. And, never just about them, but also about you and me. And because I believe there is something more to Christmas than Santa and reindeer. I wonder… What does all this mean for us today?

What does all this mean for you today? With the world as it is?

With your life as it is?

So if any of this, on some level, rings true or tugs at your heart, let me ask. With everything else already neatly in place...

If there is something in this story about *Peace on Earth* which weaves itself around some deep longing within you, how is it you are going to get ready for that kind of Christmas?

If there is something in this story about everyone having a place and not just the rich and the powerful and something in the story which brings into focus how you imagine life and world might be. Should be. How is it you are going to get ready that kind of Christmas?

If there is something in this story about *God with us* which rings true; which tugs at your spirit. God with us.

Not God over us.

Not God judging us.

Not God condemning us.

God with us in this wonderful, complex, sorrowful, joyful thing we call life.

God with you and me. God with us and them.

God here. God now.

Just as you are. Just as we are. Just as they are.

So, if there is something about this story... Something about Christmas

Which is about more than trees and gifts and carols and cards Then let me ask...

What are you doing to get ready for that kind of Christmas?

Be Careful What You Ask For

A Sermon for Advent

Prologue.

In her book *Teaching a Stone to Talk* Annie Dillard writes:

On the whole, I do not find Christians, outside of the catacombs, sufficiently sensible of conditions. Does anyone have the foggiest idea what sort of power we so blithely invoke? Or, as I suspect, does no one believe a word of it? The churches are children playing on the floor with their chemistry sets, mixing up a batch of TNT to kill a Sunday morning. It is madness to wear ladies straw hats or velvet hats to church; we should all be wearing crash helmet. Ushers should issue life preservers and signal flares; they should lash us to our pews. For the sleeping god may wake someday and take offense, or the waking God draw us out to where we can never return.

Sermon

Much to her mother's dismay, in early January 1952 my Mom got on an airplane for the first time in her life. She flew from Pittsburgh, PA to the Elmendorf Air Force Base in Anchorage, AK to marry my Dad who was stationed there during the Korean War. I was reminded of this because on the day after Thanksgiving I drove to Pittsburgh to see my Mom. After having dinner together, she ask if I would help decorate her apartment for Christmas. I pulled out her container of Christmas decorations and began putting them around her apartment. The wreath went on the door and the stuffed Santa on the floor outside her door. Her collection of snowmen found a place scattered among her pictures of her grandchildren. Finally, towards the bottom of the container and wrapped in a piece of tissue paper I found an old ornament of a child on a dog sled being pulled by a Huskie. When I asked her about it and ask if she wanted me to find a place for it, my Mom told me it was the first ornament she and my Dad bought together when they were in Alaska and the only ornament they had on first Christmas together. I cleared a space and placed it on the bookcase directly across the room from her favorite chair so she would see it each day. Christmas is like that, isn't it?

Shodie and I did our own version of that this past week.

We lifted boxes down out of the attic.

We placed candles in our upstairs windows which we do each year.

The Santa painted on a ski went to its designated spot by the front door.

Our collection of creches found their way to the mantle and the hallway table.

And, later today ornaments our children made years ago as Christmas gifts for us will be carefully lifted out of their box and lovingly hung on the tree.

Christmas is like that, isn't it?

For all those reasons and more, I love Christmas. I love…

The carols. The cards. The lights.

The decorations. The reminders.

So much of this season is like that. Wrapped up in memories. And in a hope so deep and so real and so profound we can hardly find words to put around it. That is why it is so wonderful. And sometimes so hard. Christmas is like that, isn't it?

Next Sunday in the Confirmation, the program Kathy DiBiasi and I lead for our 9th grade students as a part of their preparation for their decision about whether to join Bedford Presbyterian Church, we will give them our Christmas Quiz. It consists of 24 questions about Christmas and about what the Bible tells us about the birth of Jesus. Here are a couple of the questions.

● How did Mary and Joseph travel to Bethlehem?
Camel. Donkey. Walked. Volkswagen. Joseph walked and Mary rode a donkey.

- How many wisemen came to see Jesus? Write the correct number.

- Which animals does the Bible say were present at Jesus' birth?
Cows, sheep and goats. Cows, donkeys and sheep. Sheep and goats only. Miscellaneous barnyard animals. Lions, tigers and elephants. None of the above.

The last question on the quiz asks how many of the multiple-choice responses you think you got right. Most of the youth guess 15 or 18 out of 24. Pretty good, right? But, as we score the quiz, most only get 2 or 3 or maybe 4 or 5 correct. Once everyone gets over the shock and the shouts of disbelief die down, we then look more closely at the narratives about the birth of Jesus to see what is there. Then talk about the way tradition and story and candlelight and starlight have become wrapped around our understanding of Christmas. But Christmas is like that, isn't it?

All that is to say, that alongside all of our careful and thoughtful preparations for Christmas and the meaning we both give to it and find in it, stands the simple and often surprising, maybe even startling, witness of the Bible. So, with Annie Dillard's observation about Christians lingering in the background, these two passages – one from Isaiah and one from Mark – designated by the Lectionary to be read on this first Sunday in Advent 2017 as we, as a Christian community, begin our preparation for and our journey towards Christmas.

Isaiah 64: 1-3

O that you would tear open the heavens and come down, so that the mountains would quake at your presence—as when fire kindles brushwood and the fire causes water to boil— to make your name known to your adversaries, so that the nations might tremble at your presence! When you did awesome deeds that we did not expect, you came down, the mountains quaked at your presence.

Mark 13: 24-26

But in those days, after that suffering, the sun will be darkened, and the moon will not give its light, and the stars will be falling from heaven, and the powers in the heavens will be shaken.

Then they will see 'the Son of Man coming in clouds' with great power and glory.

O come, O come Emmanuel.

Come, thou long expected Jesus.

Be careful what you ask for.

Be careful as you say those words and sing those carols and as we, as a community of faith, do our best to be ready for God when God comes.

Or, was Annie Dillard correct.

Maybe we are like children playing on the floor with our chemistry sets mixing up a batch of TNT.

Here is what I find myself thinking about as we begin our preparations for Christmas. Besides all the wonder and the excitement and the tinsel and the holiday cheer, the Bible reminds us there is something disruptive about Christmas. Something about the coming of God which make mountains quake and the heavens shake. Something about Advent and Incarnation which turns our world...the world...this world...inside out or right side up. Something about the birth of Jesus which stands counter the traditional world view of who is in and who is out. And about what power looks like. And about who or what asks for and deserves our allegiance.

So, here is my challenge to you. During everything else you do to get ready for Christmas, pay attention to the story. Pay attention to those moments which are waiting to be transformed turning the moment you have right then *right side up*. Pay attention to where the disruptive story of Bible wants to break into the routine of your life or the headlines in the news or into the way you use your time or spend your money. Pay attention to that moment which invites you and opens you up to Incarnation or to being Incarnation.

As I said, I love Christmas.

The decorations. The carols. The cards. I even love shopping for gifts.

And, I also love the Bible.

And I take its witness seriously.

So, I am often stopped in my tracks and challenged and convicted by its witness. *Come, thou long expected Jesus.*

May the mountains and the heavens and my life and our world be shaken by your coming.

A Saint to Somebody

You can name them. Many of you already have.

Those saints who have been and are a part of your life.

Those people whose faith helped to nurture your faith. Those mentors whose values and work and witness serve as a role model for you to follow. You remember and can name those people who helped you identify and claim your own unique gifts and abilities and how you might use them to make the world a better place. Just like I can, you can still see their face and hear their voice and speak with them in your heart.

But, here's the thing. As important as that is.

And, like you, I am grateful beyond words for the impact those saints had and have on my life. Like you, I would not be who I am today or where I am today if it was not for them. As important as your recognizing their impact on your life and faith, and giving thanks for who they were and are and taking a moment to realize you are not alone, have not done it alone or become who you are alone and that you stand and live your life surrounded by that great cloud of witness...

As important as that is, it is not enough. There is also this.
You are called to be a saint to somebody.
I don't know who that somebody is.
You may not know who that somebody is.
But that is a part of the deal.
A part of who you are called to be.

Don't get me wrong.
It's not like you polish your halo and walk out the door and strut or stroll down the street or into work saying to yourself, *"I am going to be a saint to somebody today."* But it does mean this. During life exactly as it is for you with opportunities and responsibilities and cares and concerns and celebrations and children and family and work and the headlines in the news. It does mean walking out the door reminding yourself you

are called to be partners with God in God's ongoing work in the world. It does mean walking out the door with eyes and heart wide open willing to see and to embrace both the beauty and the pain. It does mean walking out the door doing your best to see and to recognize the imprint of the Holy on each person you see and meet.

You become a saint to someone in that moment you see them for who they are and help them to see themselves for who they are. You become a saint to someone by walking with them through the joys and struggles of their lives. You become a saint to someone by doing your best to put into practice the values of your faith even though more often than not you feel you fall short. You become a saint to someone by being honorable and kind and compassionate and generous. You become a saint to someone by seeing and being grace and hope and peace and light.

As Megan Hansen wrote for our Facebook page this morning: *"Being a saint comes not with angel wings, but rather work boots."* So this morning...

We remember and give thanks for all the saints. Those who have been the saints in our lives.

And, for that great cloud of witnesses which surrounds us. And for the stories they tell and the witness they bear which help us connect past to present and today to tomorrow.

And, we also remember and give thanks for this particular community of saints for who you are and for all you do. For who we are and who we are called to be.

Today, we remember and give thanks for all the saints.

You and I included.

Getting into Trouble

I grew up being taught and learning to be good.

A good boy. A good son.

A good brother. A good student. A good person.

Which, among other things, meant...

I did as I was told and did what was expected of me.

I was respectful of others. I did my best. I was polite.

I followed the rules. I didn't make waves.

And, I grew up being taught and learning to be a good Christian which meant...

Showing up to church each week. Sitting with my parents and my brothers in "our" pew. Going to Sunday School and youth groups.

Learning about the Bible.

Putting my offering in the offering plate.

Being a good Christian was fundamentally about where I was and who I was with for a couple hours on a Sunday morning.

Being good, whether at church or in school or out with my friends on a Friday or on a date on Saturday night was primarily about being nice and doing my part and not getting into trouble or causing trouble. *Being good* was and is a complement about who I was and who I am. Does any of this sound familiar?

But, here's the thing.... The *good* I was taught to be...
The polite and the respectful and the not making waves...
Doesn't always jive with the Bible which you and I claim to take seriously. Or with who Jesus was and with what Jesus taught which we claim as the example and the foundation for how we are to live.

Consider or reconsider the scripture reading for this morning. Jesus sends out the disciples to cure disease and to cast out demons. Good things, right? But to understand these verses we need to read them through their eyes and not our own. In reality, what Jesus commands the disciples to do was disruptive behavior when the cultural norm was you were not even to associate with or to include those types of people in who you were and what you did. The disciples were to raise the dead. Cleanse lepers. And in an act of repudiation and defiance shake the dust of their feet from the homes and communities which did not welcome who they were or what they were doing. Rather than being nice, Jesus tells them *"to be as wise as serpents and as innocent as doves."*

Am I misreading these verses about how disruptive this behavior and these actions were? Before you answer, consider the next several verses. The ones following on the heels of Jesus saying, *"be as wise as serpents and as innocent as doves."* Again, Jesus speaking….

Beware of them, for they will hand you over to councils and flog you in their synagogues; and you will be dragged before governors and kings because of me…Brother will betray brother to death, and a father his children, and children will rise against parents and have them put to death; and you will be hated by all because of my name. (Matthew 10: 17-18 and 21-22a)

Doesn't sound to me like *being nice* or *being good.*

All because they healed the sick and cleansed the lepers and cast out demons and proclaimed the coming of the Kingdom of God.

In his Commencement Speech to the graduates of Bates College in Maine in May 2016, John Lewis, United States Congressman and Civil Rights leader and activist and recipient of the Presidential Medal of Honor, said this:

"It was Dr. King who inspired me to stand up, to speak up and speak out. And I got in the way.

I got in trouble.

Good trouble, necessary trouble."

Growing up, whether as a person or as a Christian, my lexicon never included or permitted the word *good* and the word *trouble* to be next to each other in a single sentence. But given the state of our country and our world…

The misogyny.

The abusive and demeaning and dehumanizing rhetoric and behavior. The predisposition to violence to resolve problems.

The widening gap between those who have far more than they need and those who struggle for their daily bread.

The desperation of those who are uprooted and who flee from their homes and their communities.

Those alienation and segregation of those who are demonized because of the color of their skin, the country of their origin or the religion they practice.

Maybe what I learned needs to change.

Maybe I need to unlearn what I have spent a lifetime being taught.

All of which leads me to this question.

When was the last time you got into trouble because of what you believe? Or, because of the values of your faith?

Or, because you stood up and spoke up and got in the way?

This may sound like a rhetorical question for you, but it is, in all seriousness, a question I have been wrestling with. Me who has spent a lifetime practicing being good and who works hard at keeping people happy.

We are good at being good. We have mastered that lesson.

But that is not what we are to be about. Not who we are called to be. We are called to something more.

We are called to see the world like God sees the world.

We are called to work towards the world envisioned in the words "Thy Kingdom come." We are still called to heal the sick and to cast out demons.

We are called to stand against Death in whatever form Death takes.

We are called to shake the dust off our feet as repudiation against all that and all those who demean and defile and exclude and demonize others.

We are called to raise the dead and to practice resurrection. All of that is disruptive behavior.

Rhetorical no longer…

When was the last time you got into trouble because of your faith? One of my favorite quotes (I don't know where it is from) is this.

If they get you asking the wrong questions they don't have to worry about the answers. I don't have many answers…yet.

But I think I am beginning to ask the right questions.

This Little Light of Mine

This reminder from the insight and wisdom of JK Rowlings. (Do you recognize her name?)

She writes:

"We've all got both light and dark inside us. What matters is the part we choose to act on. That's who we really are."

And, this reminder from Jesus... *You are the light of the world.*

It is so simple.
And, so hard at the very same time.

When you are kind to another you are the light of the world.

When you stand up for what you know to be right you are the light of the world.

When you feed someone who is hungry you are the light of the world.

When you smile at a stranger you are the light of the world.

When you walk humbly with your God you are the light of the world.

When you treat another the way you would like to be treated you are the light of the world.

When you treat another the way they would like to be treated you are the light of the world.

When you extend hospitality you are the light of the world.

When you build a longer table rather than a higher wall you are the light of the world.

When you see God in the eyes of another you are the light of the world.

When you see God in your own hands and face you are the light of the world.

When your words heal you are the light of the world.

When your vision of tomorrow matches the Dream of God you are the light of the world.

When your vision of tomorrow drives your actions today you are the light of the world.

When you claim your calling as a child of God you are the light of the world.

When you include those Jesus named as the *least of these* you are the light of the world.

When you sow seeds of hope you are the light of the world.

When you build up rather than tear down you are the light of the world.

When you seek justice and resist evil you are the light of the world.

When you reach out your hand you are the light of the world.

When love wins you are the light of the world.

When the Bread of Life becomes intertwined with your life you are the light of the world.

When you understand you are the Cup of Blessing you are the light of the world.

This little light mine I'm going to let it shine.

Intimacy

While this was the message for this morning, we began our service by remembering and naming those killed in the shooting at Emanuel AME Church in Charleston, SC.

Cynthia Hurd, 54, branch manager for the Charleston County Library System

Susie Jackson, 87, longtime church member

Ethel Lance, 70, employee of Emanuel AME Church for 30 years

Rev. DePayne Middleton-Doctor, 49, admissions counselor of Southern Wesleyan University

The Honorable Rev. Clementa Pinckney, 41, state senator, Reverend of Emanuel AME Church

Tywanza Sanders, 26, earned business administration degree from Allen University

Rev. Daniel Simmons Sr., 74, retired pastor (died at MUSC)

Rev. Sharonda Singleton, 45, track coach at Goose Creek High School
Myra Thompson, 59, church member

And we remember to Dylann Storm Roof, 21 who walked into that church to kill others.

And, this reminder from William Stringfellow of who we are called to be and what we are called to do.

"In the face of death, live humanly. In the middle of chaos, celebrate the Word. Amidst Babel, speak the truth. Confront the noise and verbiage and falsehood of death with the truth and potency and efficacy of the Word of God. Know the Word, teach the Word, nurture the Word, preach the Word, define the Word, incarnate the Word, do the Word, live the Word. And more than that, in the Word of God, expose death and all death's works and wiles, rebuke lies, cast out demons, exorcise, cleanse the possessed, raise those who are dead in mind and conscience."

One of my favorite family photos sits on a table at the top of the stairs to the second floor of our home. It is a picture of me and our youngest son taken many years ago when we were on vacation at the Jersey shore. Brandon and I had been playing together in the waves. Whether just jumping over them as the broke onto the beach or riding them on one of our boogie boards, I can't remember. But in the picture we are just sitting on the beach together. Him on my lap. Me with my arms wrapped around him. Both of us watching the waves and looking together at the horizon. I like the picture for all it represents. Father. Son. Love. Contentment. Wonder. Beauty. Irreplaceable time together.

I found myself thinking about that picture as I thought about this morning.

Knowing it is Father's Day.

Knowing we would be here together.

Knowing that we are here to be reminded of that *something more*, that *something other* which we know and name as God.

And, also knowing that how we think about God and talk about God matters because it shapes something of who we are and how we see and respond to and live in the world around us.

Our language about God matters in all kinds of ways, but this morning I want to think with you about God as *Daddy* which may come as something of a surprise when I am so intentional about using inclusive language both when I read scripture and when I refer to God. But the point I want to make this morning is not about gender. Not about God as male or female. The point I want to make is about intimacy.

When I was growing up all the language, I ever heard about God was masculine and about power. Primarily power over. God as King. Lord. Heavenly Father. God above me. God over me. God demanding, controlling, caring, but distant. God all powerful. God all knowing. God as both Rule Maker and Judge. In some ways the God of my growing up may not have been all that different from the way God was portrayed and used (or misused?) in the time of Jesus. God, for Jesus and for the Jewish community of that time, was mostly confined to

Jerusalem and to the Temple and to the Holy of Holies in the Temple which could only be entered by a special priest at a specified time. God then, as God was in my growing up, was separate and apart and above and distant, and could only be approached with fear and trembling.

Then along comes Jesus.

Who refers to God not as King or Lord, but as *Abba*. Not as Ruler or Judge, but as *Daddy* or *Papa*.

With the language he uses to speak about God, Jesus pulls God out of the Temple and out of the church and away from the priests and pastors and bishops and popes and into and alongside your life and mine.

If I am right about Jesus

And, if Jesus is right about God...

Then, what God desires is an intimacy with us which, at least for me, resembles the picture at the top of our stairs of my arms wrapped around my son. As a father, maybe better...as a *Daddy*...I know what that moment felt like and feels like. And, as a father I know what that moment meant and still means.

So, what about you?

What picture or memory captures a similar intimacy for you as my picture does for me? It can be a memory of you and your child?

Or you and your grandchild? Or, you and your partner?

Or, you and a friend?

What I would like you to remember is what that moment felt like and feels like to you.

Trust. Contentment. Safety. Openness. Honesty.

You, for a moment, at your best.

The world, for a moment, just right.

And then I invite you to take a step back.

And to look at your own life.

And to consider that what you remember and know of that special moment.

For that moment is like what God longs for with you and for you.

This I Believe

A Sermon for Confirmation Sunday

This I believe.

I believe there is *Something More*. *Something More* than you and me. *Something More* than us and them.

Something More that is above us and beneath us and around us and in us.

Something More that is that connective thread which links your life to mine and our lives to theirs. And links the past to the present and the present to the future.

I don't know its full name.

I learned to call it God and learned about it as I learned about Jesus.

And, that name is comfortable for me and makes sense to me and carries meaning for me, but I have come to believe it is known by other names as well.

Yahweh. Jehovah. Adonai. Allah.

Ground of our Being. Lord.

King. Creator. Spirit.

Each name carries with it some insight and some understanding lovingly and carefully added by the searching and experience of our forebears and by the wisdom of the ages. But whatever name we use and whatever understanding we have only captured only a small piece of that *Something More*.

And, while there is much about that which I know and name as God I do not know and may never know, here is what I think I do know.

That *Something More* I know as God is fundamentally about…

Compassion and kindness.

Hope and goodness.

And about all having enough and all having a place.

And that which I know and name as God stands against…

Violence and prejudice and hatred and bigotry.

And all that would demean or diminish or destroy another human being. This I believe.

But here is where you have to be careful…
Which I hope you won't be.
The moment you begin to believe that any of what I just said is true.
The moment you begin to take seriously and to make space in your life for that which we know and name as God, it turns your life inside out.

Literally.

Here is what I mean.

While our understanding of God is often deeply personal, it is not meant to be private.

God calls us to live from the inside out.
From what we know of God and of that which gives our life meaning and depth and direction out in the wonder and complexity of the world as it is.

I believe you and I are called to be the presence of God. To be the eyes and hands and heart of God. In those places where we are each day and with those and to those who come and go in our life each day. Not just with those who are our friends and those with whom we feel comfortable, but maybe even more important God to those who aren't.

As the hands and heart of God, we are called to be and called to make the choice to be hope and kindness and compassion and comfort. We are called to stand against violence and bigotry and that which harms another.

All of which is easy to say, but not always so easy to do. How are you kind to those who are hateful or mean? How are you hope when all you see or feel are challenges or problems? How do you stand against violence when the risk is the violence will be turned towards you?

Nothing you do may be more difficult…or more important.

We are to live from the inside out.

As the heart and hands of God in the world.

And, finally this.

I believe in you. All of you. Confirmands especially. Because I know this.

I cannot do or believe any of this all on my own. I need your presence. I count on your questions. I rely your vision. You challenge me to live up to what I say I believe.

I need you to remind me that *"I don't know."* as an easy and convenient way to avoid the question or a challenging situation is not only the one response I will not allow in Confirmation. It is also not an acceptable response when I lift my head and open my eyes and do my best to see both the wonder and complexity of the world around me. Maybe that is why we are here together. Why *church* is important. A small place where we can remind each other and help each other and encourage each other and challenge each other to turn in the direction of that *Something More* which we know and name as God and practice here that we might risk being compassion and kindness and justice out there.

This I believe.

Looking in the Right Places

An Easter Sermon

Let's be honest.

Or, at least accurate.

Easter didn't begin with the triumph with which we began our service this morning. It begins in the dark.

For both then and now, the headlines in the news were and are more about crucifixion than resurrection. And life for too many still gets swallowed up by sorrow. And hopes continue to be dashed and dreams shattered whether by cross or by circumstance. We all know something of how that darkness feels. That being the case, we also know something of how those women felt who stumbled their way to the tomb of Jesus on that Sunday morning so long ago.

Shoulders slumped. Eyes glazed over.

More empty than full. More broken than whole.

Who, with tears in their eyes, willed themselves back to that Jewish cemetery.

They made their way there at some risk to themselves and in open defiance of the authorities who had crucified Jesus. But, despite the risk, they were determined to pay their last respects and to do what must be done in order to provide for a proper burial in their love-filled effort to counterbalance the shame and the horror associated with a Roman crucifixion. We can discuss and debate what happened in that moment when they arrived at the tomb or when that moment actually was, but that is not the point of the story and would only serve as a convenient distraction to what is really being asked and what is really at stake. The story turns on the haunting question asked of the women as they stood before that tomb with tears in their eyes. *"Why do you look for the living among the dead?"*

Knowing Easter was coming…

And that I would be here, and you would be there,

I have been thinking about and asking myself that question for several weeks now.

And, truth be told, I have probably been thinking about and wrestling with that question in some way, shape or form for even longer than that.

"Why do you look for the living among the dead?"

It is the ultimate Easter question.

Posed first to the women… And then…

And now…

To you and to me.

Why do you look for the living among the dead? Why do YOU look for the living among the dead?

The challenge for us in moments like this…

And maybe, to one degree or another, in all the moments of our life…

Is to decide whether to trust that what we know of the Easter story is true. True not just, or ever primarily about, what did or did not happen to Jesus, but true that somehow in God's grand scheme of things…

That crucifixion does not have the final word.

That violence does not have the final word. That hate and fear do not have the final word.

That betrayal and failure do not have the final word. That Death does not have the final word.

And, to decide, too, whether resurrection is possible.

And whether out of the chaos and craziness we sometimes experience in our own lives and see in the world around us, Life, in a way we could not imagine before, can and does emerge anew around us and within us.

The Easter question is this:

Beyond trumpets and flowers and bonnets and eggs and bunnies and baskets, and, face to face with sorrow and brokenness and despair and death…
Can you hold onto…
Can you turn towards…
Can you believe in…
A hope like that?

But even then…

Even doing our best to hold onto that hope, we are still left with the question, "What next?" Against all odds and evidence to the contrary, what does it mean for you and for me to turn around and to seek the living?

Here is what I think I know.

It is not here, it's somewhere out there.

It is not wrapped up in you or me, it's somewhere out there.

Somehow seeking the living means stepping out into that world that crucified Jesus and continues to crucify people still.

It means caring and compassion.

It means seeing and naming and knowing those whom Jesus referred to as the least of these.

It means praying deeply, not for things or about things, but praying deeply enough that you find an intimacy with God that then nurtures courage enough and strength enough to live with an intimacy with others.

It means gratitude and grace deep enough that it humbles you.

It means refusing to turn away from the cross.

Refusing to turn away from the violence.

Refusing to turn away from that which demeans or demonizes or destroys another and instead doing what you can;

Doing all you can;

To build peace and to bend that long arc of history in the direction of justice.

I may or may not do any of that very well, but my deepest convictions and my faith at its best tells me what I just said to you is true.

Now the truth is I can't prove any of this to you.

I can't prove Life is stronger than Death.

I can't prove hope overcomes despair.

I can't prove gratitude matters.

I can't prove compassion is the way to life.

I can't prove that new life can emerge from all that would entomb you and me.

I can't prove that sense of something of Jesus alive and with us still.

I can't prove God has the final word.

All I know for sure is this. You and I have a choice.

A choice about which direction we will face and about which fundamental values will guide and shape our choices and our decisions. A choice about narrative around which you will build your life.

So, as you consider the Gospel and the wild, life-changing claims of Easter, Consider also your own life…

Your own hopes and dreams.

Your own vision for what tomorrow might bring…not just for you, and your household. Not just for those who look like you and talk like you and live like you, but for all who fall within the circle of God's love which, in the end, is each one of us.

In your estimation what does have the final word? Life or death?

In your estimation, surrounded as we are by those who still crucify and that which still entombs us, does hope endure and is new life possible?

In your estimation, are the wild whispers of faith which surround the Easter which we remember and retell today idle tales or profound good news?

You decide.

On the first day of the week at early dawn, the women came to the tomb bringing the spices they had prepared only find the stone rolled back and to be confronted by the ultimate question of Easter. *"Why do you seek the living among the dead?"*

Serious Stuff

So, this morning, these challenging (at least to me!) words from Matthew's Gospel:

> *Then Jesus told his disciples, "If any want to become my followers, let them deny themselves and take up their cross and follow me. For those who want to save their life will lose it, and those who lose their life for my sake will find it. For what will it profit them if they gain the whole world, but forfeit their life? Or what will the give in return for their life?"*

Jesus probably didn't say this. The writer of Matthew's gospel probably put these words in the mouth of Jesus as instruction to the early Christian community to whom he was writing. But the image here is stark. *Taking up your cross* didn't mean shouldering the burdens and challenges and sorrows that come with life as we know it which is how some today read and interpret and understand these verses. Those to whom these words were first addressed *carrying your cross* was a concrete and awful reality. The Roman authorities crucified not just Jesus. They crucified thousands. Those who were forced to *carry their cross*, literally, carried them on their way to their own execution.

Serious stuff if we take the Bible seriously.

So, what are we to do with passages like this? Before you run for the doors or cover your ears, and because some part of all this is to be good news and not guilt news; guidance and encouragement for who we might be and how we might live. let me tell you what I think this passage means.

The problem with Jesus which got him into trouble with the *powers that be,* both religious and political, was that his vision of the world was fundamentally different from theirs. He constantly pushed beyond the carefully prescribed and tacitly agreed upon social and religious and political boundaries in almost everything he said and did.

Instead of God being locked in the Temple and accessible only through prescribed rituals and sacrifices and religious leaders, he talked and taught about an intimacy with God. And referred to God using the word which means *Daddy or Papa.*

He touched and healed and included and shared meals with those who everyone else deemed as sinful or unclean or dangerous or aliens or enemies and told everyone else they should do the same and that if they didn't, they were turning their backs on God.

He talked about God's Kingdom come. Not after you die or on some distant day, but God's Kingdom come right here and right now. Any time and any place where compassion and kindness and welcome and hospitality are extended and received.

He talked about God's Kingdom and not Rome's empire.

He talked about the peace of God and not Pax Romana, and about peacemaking more than peacekeeping.

He talked about all having enough and all having a place in a time and place where most did not have enough, and most did not have a place and there was little to no hope with the way things were that it would ever be different.

He talked about allegiance to God and not allegiance to Caesar.

He said compassion was more important than following the rules.

He continued to speak up when they told him to be quiet.

He reached out to others when they told him to keep his hands to himself.

And all that is what got him into trouble.

And, in the end, because of politics and pressure and potential unrest, he was forced to carry a cross.

That's all well and good. And all about Jesus.

But where does that leave you and me? Here I think.

This passage is not about martyrdom, but about fearlessness. It is not about self-denial, but about self-control.

It is not about asceticism, but about seeing how our lives might be lived in partnership with God and God's ongoing work in the world.

Here is what I mean.

The values wrapped up in God's Kingdom come; the values and witness taught and testified to by Jesus come with a cost.

Hope comes with a cost.

Peace comes with a cost.

Compassion comes with a cost.

Kindness comes with a cost.

Welcoming the stranger and the disenfranchised comes with a cost.

New life comes with a cost.

A cost measured in terms of: Time. Energy. Commitment. Sorrow. Hard work. Frustration. Finances. Fatigue.

A cost measured in terms of your life and mine.

The question before us always is:

Are we willing to accept that cost?

Are we willing to spend ourselves on compassion?

Are we willing to be fearless in building hope?

Are we willing to risk ourselves or something of ourselves setting aside self-interest for the sake of another?

Are we willing to give up something; to say *No* to something so that another might, at least, have what is needed?

Are we willing to lose your life walking towards peace?

The witness of the Gospel is this.

If we do; When we do;

Then, we will find our lives and begin to live.

Be Jesus

Despite what you have heard or might have of heard, or been taught at some time in the past;

I want to tell you today that… It is not about…

Consubstantiation.

Or, transubstantiation.

Or, any other type of *substantiation*, if there is another type.

And, it is not about…

Christology.

Or, eschatology.

Or, soteriology.

Or, ecclesiology.

Or, any other *ology* you would like to add.

And, it is not about…

Hypostatic union.

Or, dispensationalism.

Or, pretribulation.

Or, predestination.

It is also not about…

Immutability.

Or, infallibility.

Or, substitutionary atonement.

Or, regeneration.

And, it is not about…

Doctrine.

Or, dogma.

Or, sanctification.

Or, purity.

It is not about…

The Trinity.

Or, the immaculate conception.

Or, walking on water.

Or, even turning water into wine.

It is about Jesus.

Healing.

Teaching.

Touching.

Challenging those who *lord it over others* in any one of 1000 different ways.

It is about Jesus.

Changing the lives of those who came in touch with him then. And, those who come in touch with him even now.

And, it is about us…

About you and me…

Doing our best to *be Jesus* in those places where we live and work each day.

To be healing.

To be hope. To be light.

To be compassion. To be challenge.

Doing our best and, each day, striving to do better:

To love God and to love our neighbor.

To turn towards and not away from those whom Jesus names as *the least of these.*

To treat others as we ourselves would like to be treated.

Here is what I mean.

When Jesus broke the bread with his disciples and passed around the cup from which they were to drink, he was not talking about sacrifice – his life for our sins like it was some God given trade-off.

Jesus was talking about presence.

About who he was now being a part of who they were. So, they could begin to do…

Would begin to do…

What they had seen and watched him do.

So, let me ask you this…

What is it about Jesus which most inspires you or challenges you or comforts you or sustains you?

What is it about Jesus that you *get* the best?

Start there.

Take that one part;

That one thing;

And, do your best to do that.

And, to be that.

To *be Jesus*…the best you can.

And So, It Is Christmas

A Sermon for Christmas Eve

And, so it is Christmas. At least, almost.

And, here we are... Together in this place.

Gathered with family and friends to sing the carols and to soak in the beauty and for a moment, at least, to allow the light of a candle to be the light which lights our way. Here in this place and on this night maybe you can step aside from the whirlwind rush of the season to be reminded, again, that Christmas is about something more than Santa and reindeer and stockings hung by the chimney with care. And, about something more than gift getting and gift giving and holiday cheer.

I like to believe, and I hope it is true...

That we have found our way here because there is something about the story we tell...

The story of a pregnant young woman and a journey to Bethlehem and the birth of a child;

The story about shepherds in the field abiding and angels appearing;

The story about either the wild-eyed craziness or absolute wisdom it takes to see and then to follow a star.

I like to believe, and I hope it is true that all this touches something... Some hope;

Some dream;

Some deep longing within you;

That turns you, again, in the direction of Bethlehem...wherever Bethlehem might be for you this day.

And, for whatever the reason...

Carols. Candles. Quiet. Story.

That you want to be here. Maybe even, need to be here.

So, what can I tell you about Christmas that you don't already know?

Or don't already dream about or hope for in the deepest and best part of your being?

That the brash dream of *Peace on Earth* is a dream worth holding onto and worth working for in our families and in our communities; To say nothing of our country and our world? Not just for your sake or my sake, but for all our sakes, as well?

That the promise of a God who comes to mix it up with your life and mine is a game changer? For now, there is something fundamentally holy about our very human lives? Something about who we are and the time we have, even those times when we feel the most ordinary or the time feels like the most routine, which partakes of the Eternal?

That the long arc of history does bend in the direction of justice and hope if we do our part. Do what we can to bend it in that way?

All this from this simple story of the birth of a child who, later in his life, would remind us that the at the very heart of who we are and how we are to live together are two wonderfully simple and incredibly challenging bits of wisdom.

First, love God.

Second, love your neighbor.

And, all these years later we continue to do our best to figure out what that means when we get up each morning and as we go to bed each night.

And, so it is Christmas. At least, almost.

So, pay attention. Hold it close.

Allow it all to sink in. Deeply.

Because it is Christmas. At least, almost.

And as you do, here my Christmas wish for you.

May you recognize the everyday angels who appear who continue to brush up against your life and who wait for you to say your own *Yes* to that grand dream of God.

May you catch a glimpse of the stars which still shine in the darkness and which still show the way.

May you refuse to give up and may you continue to make that long journey in the direction of peace.

May you recognize the giftedness and the holiness that is a part of your life…and a part of the lives of everyone else whom you see and meet. Never in your life have you met a mere mortal.

May you make room in your life for the God who comes. Who comes to be with you and for you, and not just above you?

May you, for a moment, take a deep breath and look around and allow the wonder and the beauty and the mystery of it all to sink deeply into your heart and mind and soul.

And, so it is Christmas.

Which Star?

A Sermon for Epiphany

We tend to read and to think of the stories describing the birth of Jesus like they are one continuous, unified narrative. Like the authors of Matthew and Luke sat down together and said, "I will tell this part of the story and you tell that part." But that is not what happened. And even though we read them together on Christmas Eve and push them together in our creches and cards, the narratives around the birth of Jesus are distinctly different and deserve to stand and to be thought about on their own. The account in Luke has one cast of characters. Matthew has another. Luke includes Caesar Augustus, Joseph and Mary, angels and shepherds and Jesus in a manger.

Matthew has none of that.

Instead, Matthew's Gospel the primary actors are a star. And, strangers from the East.

And Herod.
Frightened (read scared to death) by the arrival and the question of the magi.

In the part of the story we read as we began our worship,

Joseph is non-existent. Mary is passive.

Jesus barely mentioned.

There is no arduous journey to Bethlehem while pregnant.

No angels in the sky. No shepherds in the field. No Jesus in a manger.

And, while we didn't read it this morning (and don't often read it because we want to keep the Christmas narrative wonderful and beautiful and miraculous), for the sake of this morning and what I found myself thinking about as I read and reread this story, I realized we also need to pay attention to what comes next in Matthew's gospel.

When the wisemen don't return to Jerusalem as he instructed them to do, Herod becomes enraged. He sends in his soldiers to slaughter all the children under the age of two in and around Bethlehem while Joseph and Mary and Jesus run for their lives. This, also, is a part of the Christmas story.

Here is the tension.

And, ultimately, the choice Matthew's Gospel presents.

On one side are these strangers from the East who come looking for Jesus. Who, if you remember the earlier part of the story when Joseph is about to dismiss Mary because she is pregnant, an angel appears telling him not to do that and informing him the child, when born, will be called and known as *Immanuel* which means *God with us*. On the other side of this story is Herod who slaughters all the children in a desperate effort to kill that same child, *Immanuel*, in order to maintain his power and control. Got it?

Which leads me to this question.

Which star do you see, and which star will you follow?

I know the way we often think about this story is that somehow, suddenly this wondrous, mysterious, miraculous star appears in the sky. All sorts of possible explanations have been offered about what that star might have been. Halley's comet. A unique alignment of planets or stars. A new star suddenly appearing and then disappearing. Personally, I love the imagery. But this year I realized maybe none of that is important or what this narrative is about. And to spend our time talking about how and why and what the possibilities might have been only serves as a distraction to keep us from grappling with what the real point and message of the story.

You see, what I realized in reading and thinking about this story again this year is there were and there are many stars in the sky. Many stars we might see and follow.

Herod saw clearly and was following his star.

His star was power, and control maintained by intimidation and brute force. But there were and are other stars, as well.

There is the star of *win at all costs*.

Or, the star of *pulling ourselves up by our own bootstraps*. Or, the star of *me first*.

Or, the star of *I deserve this*. Or, the star of *I can't do that*. Or, *what if we fail*.

Or, *I am only one person*.

All those stars are there in the sky and the narratives they represent surround us. They flow through the air we breathe and are in the water we drink. They are the stories we were told as we grew up.

Which star will you see, and which star will you follow?

And then you come to church. And here, you are reminded… Here we are reminded… There is another story. Another narrative.

Another star in the sky we might see and follow. This star has something to do with *God with us*. With each and every one of us.

This star has something to do with treating others as we and they would like to be treated. This star has something to do with the last being first and a table big enough for all. This star has something to do being peacemakers and peace on earth. This star has something to do with light and grace and welcome and resurrection.

No wonder Herod was afraid.

Those Magi with their question and that star which they saw and chose to follow called into question EVERYTHING he had built his life around.

And because we believe the Bible is not just about then, but also about now. And not just about them, but also about you and me. The question which confronted both Herod and the Magi is now asked of you and me.

Which star will you see, and which star do you follow?

Let me end with this.

What I often say when I finish reading a portion of scripture on Sunday mornings.

May the same Spirit which inspired the Gospel writer to record these words help interpret their meaning for our lives this day.

If You See Something Say Something

When we meet on Sunday afternoon with the young adults who participate in our Confirmation program, one of the challenges Kathy DiBiasi and I face as we talk with them about God and Jesus and the difference between faith and religion, is how to read and understand the Bible. They are so used to reading textbooks – history books and science books or current event articles – and learning or memorizing what they read so they can play it back on quizzes or tests that they try to do the same thing with the Bible. We try to encourage them to read the Bible for meaning and not like a science book or the newspaper. One of the ways we do this is we will give them Robert Frost's poem *The Road Less Traveled*. You probably know it. It begins like this.

Two road diverged in a yellow wood, and sorry I could not travel both
And be one traveler, long I stood
And looked down one as far as I could to where it bent in the undergrowth.

And it ends with these two lines.

I took the one less traveled by,
And that has made all the difference.

We give them the poem, ask them to read it and then ask them to share with us what it means. There is usually an awkward pause of some sort as they try figure out what the poem has to do with God or Jesus or church or faith, because that is usually the *default/go to* answer for questions like this which are asked by the Pastor or the Director of Educational Ministries. But they finally get around to telling us the poem is about what choice you will make and what path you will follow. Then, having gotten them that far, we give them a Bible and ask them to turn to Genesis 1. The very first words in the Bible.

In the beginning when God created the heavens and the earth, the earth was a formless void and darkness covered the face of the deep. Then God said, Let there be light," and there was light. And there was evening and there was morning, the first day.

Once they have found their way to that page in the Bible, we ask them to read through the entire chapter and then to tell us what it means. We give them this hint. It is not about creation. Trusting you can do at least two things at the same time, if you want to read through Genesis 1 yourself to while I continue feel free to do so. Just remember. It is not about creation.

Here is some background which is important as you read through or think about these verses and as you seek to understand the Bible.

The Bible was not written front to back. The authors didn't sit down and start with page one and work their way forward. The Bible was, in fact, written backwards. Authors looking back from transformative moments – the Exodus in Hebrew Scripture or the resurrection in Christian scripture – and creating a narrative to give meaning to what they had experienced.

Genesis 1 was written sometime around the middle of the 5th century BCE at the time the Babylonian exile which was an existential crisis point in Jewish history. All the touchstones they turned to and relied on to identify themselves as God's Chosen People – land, King, Temple, Torah – had been lost or destroyed. Life and faith and identity were in chaos. During all that uncertainty, the authors and compilers of the Hebrew Bible wrote these opening verses.

If I oversaw putting the Bible together. I would call these opening verses a Prologue and not Chapter 1 because these words, at least for me, inform the whole rest of the narrative.

So, where is all this going? To get there, back to the question Kathy and I ask the Ninth Graders in Confirmation.

What do these verses mean?

For me they read as a *Statement of Faith*.
The world is chaotic and broken. Formless. A void. Dark.

And, in that darkness and brokenness and void God creates bringing order to the chaos. And, not just creates, declares what is made *good*.

Light. Dark. Day. Night. Sea monsters. Creeping things. All good.

Then, humankind created in God's own image.
Male and female created in God's own image.

And God saw what God had made and behold it was not just good, but very good.

I don't know about you, but the world does not feel very good or very orderly to me right now.

Beyond the relentless day in/day out swirl of craziness two headlines particularly gave me pause this week. The first is that there were 11 school shootings in the first 23 days of January. One every other day. The second was an article wondering if we even care about such events anymore.

We are drowning...
I am drowning...
In bad news and brokenness and heartache and heartbreak.
So here is what I did.

I went on Facebook and asked for people to tell me where they had seen or experienced kindness this week. Or, seen people treating others decently. And, people responded. Here is what they said.

I like this question... it makes me consider again the woman who smiled at me and made a nice comment as I waited for her to get out of her car so I could get in mine. And the woman who said hello to all the staff of the coffee shop when she walked in. And to appreciate even more all the people who took the time to wish me well after surgery. Small acts but taken together they help to make each interaction more human and make each day more connected.

In Katonah when I want to grab a quick bite I either go to Goldberg's Deli or the Pizza Station. Most staff in those two places are all Latino (mostly Guatemalan) and I am consistently welcomed and engaged in conversation that feels like something more than small talk. Being comforted by the opportunity to speak Spanish in those situations reminds me of the hospitality and community that seems to emanate from Latino culture and families. And the grace they display all the while facing unjust immigration reform. It makes me stop and think. If only solving the problem were as easy as interacting at the deli.

Grocery store; smiles & friendly comments to a mom with loud kids. Post Office; a man held the door for me & others.

Cars who slow down when going by my puppy and I on the road. Trying not to scare her.

I am so grateful that I see it (almost) every day at work. And I love every reminder for random acts of kindness, so thank you for that, and the thoughtful question!

A man on my walk to work yesterday gave me the brightest and warmest of smiles as we passed each other on the street. Instead of avoiding eye contact, we both briefly exchanged a sense of our shared humanity.

In the chaos of a NYC store, my daughter lost her purse. The young man who found it, texted her and It was returned to her within a couple of hours.

My 5-year-old daughter giving friends, teachers and us hugs.

I saw an older woman who walks with a cane kneel down to hold a toddler at bay so that his mother could focus on getting her bike off the train.

At the Atlanta airport the folks were super kind when my wife lost her boarding pass. Also, the orphans in Mexico were incredibly kind and patient with us Americans who don't know their language.

So here is what feels like truth to me.
There are huge issues out there.
Just as there have always been.
Some seem to be getting better, but others are getting worse.
Racism. Poverty. Misuse and abuse of power whether in governments or in the workplace. Opioids. Hunger. Whatever was above the fold on the front page of whatever newspaper you glanced at this morning. We ignore those issues at our own peril.

But there is also this.

The older woman with the cane who kneels down to hold the hand of a toddler.

The stranger who smiles when you pass on the street.

The little girl who wants to give you a hug.

Those everyday kindnesses which grace your life.

Maybe all this is my own Statement of Faith.

I believe there is more goodness in the world than evil.

And, while not the solution to everything between us and God's Kingdom come, certainly a place we can begin is with those everyday kindnesses and goodness, and those moments of decency and respect which punctuate the lives of most of us each day. So, don't turn away from the hard work which is ours to do. But, also, know and name and embody the goodness which the Bible claims is built into your very DNA. And, share that goodness with others awakening theirs in them.

And, when you see something, say something.

Notice the hug of a child and the couple walking down the street holding hands. Pay attention the kindness of a stranger and the door held for another. And, say something. At least to yourself so you stop long enough to see clearly those life-giving moments which grace your day that you might remember how and who you were created to be.

Then turn and be that for another.

Two Words for Christmas

I don't know about you, but I need Christmas this year. Maybe more than ever.

But, this year, I need Christmas to be more than the carols and the candles. I need it to be more than the gifts that await our giving and receiving.

I even need it to be more than our being here on Christmas Eve. As wonderful and as beautiful as all that is.

In a world seemingly turned upside down by hatred and violence, this year I need Christmas to really be Christmas. I need its message of *Peace on Earth* and *God with us* to be more than a card we send or receive. And more than a refrain in the carols we sing. I need the words and that message of Christmas to stack up around my life and to shake and shape me to the core. And because I long for the world to be different than it is and better than it is not just for you and me, but for all the children of earth, I need those words and that message to prop up my courage and to strengthen my resolve. I need that Christmas hope to hang on to and to turn me in the direction I need to go. I need Christmas to be Christmas this year and not just another Hallmark holiday. So, if you are at all like me and the dream wrapped up in the promises of Christmas tugs at your heart and mind and soul, I have two words to offer to you this Christmas.

Not *Merry Christmas.* Not *Happy Holidays.*

Not *Silent Night* or Mary and Joseph or Jesus and Bethlehem.

What I have to offer are the two words whispered by those heavenly sent angels.

Words first whispered to Mary's cousin Elizabeth and to her husband, Zechariah, and then to Mary and then to Joseph and finally to the shepherds in their fields abiding. Two words which, as they took them to heart, changed their lives.

Our Christmas memories and traditions soften the harsh reality of the story. Mary and Joseph and Elizabeth and the shepherds were just ordinary people living in an occupied land dominated by a foreign power and struggling each day just to get by. To have enough food and to find enough work and to maintain their sense of who they were amidst the hardships and challenges of life. It was to the likes of them the angels came.

And, now all these years later, those same two words are whispered again waiting for you and me to hear them. And, if we dare…to take them to heart.

Two words which stand counter to everything you see or read in the news. Two words up against all those other words. All that shouting. All that hatred. All that bigotry. *"Fear Not."* Those God sent angels say.

"Fear not."

Can you believe it? With the world as it is?

Two words for Christmas which turned their world and ours upside down or maybe, just maybe, turned it right side up.

That is not to say there is not craziness in the world out there. Or terrorism. Or violence. Or hatred.

All that is real. All too real.

The question is how will you live in response to it?

The *fear not* of the angels did not gloss over the harsh reality of the world in which Mary and Joseph lived and into which Jesus was born. The *fear not* of the angels was a call and a challenge for them to live their lives differently. To live their lives not dominated by fear, but instead to live their lives believing that a different day was possible.

When fear takes hold of your life it soon festers and becomes anger and hatred and suspicion and vengeance. You point fingers. You blame them. They become not quite human to you. They deserve what they get or what you can dish out.

But Gandhi was right when he said, *"An eye for an eye will leave the whole world blind."*

The Christmas story reminds us of something else.

Promises something more.

It tells us there might be another way.

That God imagines another way.

That anxiousness and anger and fear when converted becomes hope. And that hope enables us to see our lives and their lives differently and to begin to build a world that will be different tomorrow than it was today.

A couple of weeks ago, on a Sunday morning, I asked those who were here with me to close their eyes and to imagine what the world might be like. This evening, here in the beauty and quiet of this space, I invite you to do the same. If the promises wrapped up in Christmas are real, what would our world look like and be like.

Can you see it?

Can you imagine it?

If you can then the question becomes:

This Christmas, what can you do to make that world which you can already see THE world in which we all live?

"Fear not," the angel said. *"I bring you good news of great joy."*

Indeed, good news of great joy!

This evening, may you hear and claim those brave words for your life and for our world.

For after all, it is Christmas.

All the People

You may remember this from when you were younger (with hand motions).

Here is the church.

Here is the steeple.

Open the door and see all the people.

On this Sunday morning...

When we return from family vacations and summer travels...

When many of you move from the more relaxed pace of summer and step back in the normal, and often, more rushed routines of fall...

Maybe even return from the restless wanderings of our spirit that in the past kept us from places like this, but which now draws us to places like this.

On this day when we...

Celebrate the beauty of the work done this summer and express our appreciation for those who helped make it happen, and...

Anticipate the arrival of a new organ this fall, and... Remember the generosity that has made it all possible... I want you to remember this...

Here is the church. There are the steeples.

But, open the door and see all the people.

For, even in this moment when we gaze in wonder at the work that was done and drink in the beauty of this incredible space, in the end...

Our primary business is not to preserve historic buildings...even though we have been blessed to be able to do so.

Our primary business is not to be a concert hall...even though we have been blessed with a building with incredible acoustics and look forward to the addition of a magnificent instrument. Our primary business is not churches or steeples.

Our primary business is to open the door and to be the people. God's Chosen people...the Bible reminds us.

God's Royal priesthood. God's Holy nation. God's Peculiar People. Can these words...

Do these words...

Might these words...

Somehow describe you and me?

Somehow describe the ministry and mission of this congregation?

God's Chosen People...not to be separate from or apart from, but those who willingly step forward to be partners with God in God's ongoing work in the world. Seeking justice. Loving kindness. Walking humbly with God.

God's Royal Priesthood...not to be elite, but to seek ways and strive for ways that our lives are perceived as a blessing to others so that, for a moment at least, those with whom we come in contact, sense something of God in our midst.

God's Holy Nation...not as distant or better than, but as those who constantly seek to discern the signs of God and the work of God during the demands of the everyday.

God's Peculiar People...who wants to be peculiar when we all work so hard just to fit in? I wonder...

Is it possible?

Maybe you wonder, as well.

But the phone call comes asking if we can help. A summer program is needed for Hispanic kids in Mt. Kisco because parents work two or three jobs to make ends meet and we say, "Yes, we will help." A neighbor is sick and needs some help. Food. Something fixed. A ride to the store. With no questions asked and without thinking twice you set aside what you are doing and step forward to help. Is there not blessing somehow in moments like that...both for them and for us?

When we risk praying for each other, risk caring for each other, and risk celebrating with each other. When we practice hospitality making space in our midst for those who would come...those who believe and those who don't believe and those who are not sure what to believe. Are those moments holy moments that hold the possibility of touching both our lives and theirs?

Every month a Midnight Run...

Every month work for Habitat for Humanity...

Twice this summer work in Hurley, Virginia...

Last winter work on the community center in Puerto Cabazis, Nicaragua...

Opportunities to help, but one that forces those who participate to grapple with the ensuing questions and confusion and soul search that results and are challenged to see life and world and God from a new and broader perspective. In such moments do we witness to what we believe and open ourselves to a new witness that can shape and change our lives?

Is this not something of who we are?

And something of who we are called to be?

Doing our best in the moment at hand, but also knowing that where we are today is, in the end, not where God would have us be.

The peculiar people of a peculiar God who forever plunges into the fray and who continually calls us forward towards that day that is yet to be...

When swords are beat into plowshares...

When the hungry finally have enough to eat...

When the Valley of the Shadow of Death is flooded with light...

When we recognize that there is only one race and that's humankind...

And between now and then God calls us to risk more. To care more. To do more. To be more.

For God's sake...

And the sake of the world God loves so much.

So, on this wonderful Sunday when we have so much to celebrate and so much to be thankful for remember this.

Here is the church.

Here is the steeple.

Open the doors and see all the people.

Amazing Grace

There he sat. Nameless. Faceless.

All but forgotten.

His beggar's cloak the same color as the dust.

In an indistinguishable heap alongside the road.

Disheveled outside. Shriveled up inside.

Hardly human to others. And, even worse, hardly human to himself.

And so, the story of one blind man's encounter with Jesus begins.

A story that in a few short sentences poses a whole host of questions…
About miracles. About what it means to really "see" or to be "blind"?
And, who is it that sees? And, who is blind?

About what the relationship is between being healed and being cured?

About who those nameless and faceless and forgotten ones are who
are still passed by each day?

About how we continue to treat some as clean and others as not clean?
Some as whole and others as "not whole"?

Some as acceptable and others as not acceptable?

And about faith? Or, faith enough?

But, back to the Bible for a moment…

There he sat as he had sat for God knows how long until that day when
Jesus happened by. Then something snapped within him or
reawakened within him. How you describe what happened depends on
where you stand in the story.

And this forgotten and nameless and faceless man suddenly shouts out and shouts out again even when told to sit down and shut up. And, when called by Jesus and against almost every social expectation religious custom imaginable...

He pushes back the hood that for so long had hidden his face and kept him nameless. He throws off his cloak which had for so long covered up his humanity.

He stumbles towards Jesus until they stood face to face...

Sightless eyes staring into Almighty eyes.

Then, these words...

These... Improbable. Paradoxical. Life changing words.

"Your faith, not me, has made you well."

And, if we believe that the somewhere in this ancient story there is some word meant to be heard today...

What word is there that you and I might hear?

Where does sacred text turn into human encounter?

Where do the issues raised by this story get played out in the world today?

Could this be the story of those like...?

Rosa Parks who refused to move to the rear of the bus?

Of Martin Luther King, Jr. who refused to be silent in the face of injustice? Of Nelson Mandela who spends his life in jail?

Or, a story about the people of El Salvador, or Nicaragua, or the Balkans?

Anyone of a million and one nameless persons? Or any one of a hundred forgotten people who suddenly cry out and stand up claiming, maybe for the first time, their own humanity and then demanding that we recognize the same?

But maybe that is the easy way to hear the story. The harder way is to think about you and me...

Because for us, it is not the poverty or race or discrimination

It is not the oppression or starvation, or illness of some sort.

That leads to our blindness...

Or, our inability to see our own humanity or the humanity of others.

But it may be this...

It may be our compulsion to busyness that blinds us to opportunities to care.

It may be the subtle arrogance that we pull over our heads that leaves little room for new learning or understanding or seeing life and world from a large perspective.

It may be the affluence that we wrap around our lives that tends to stifle both genuine gratitude and compassion.

The question that maybe we most need to ask is this: When and how are we like blind Bartimaeus?

What hood do we need to push back from our face in order to see? What cloak do we need to unwrap from around our lives?

How might we need to stumble towards God?

How is it that we might have faith enough to begin to see?

In the end, maybe what this story tells us is that we are not human until we are human together and that blindness is not just about our eyes, but also about our hearts and minds.

The Dream of Christmas

Blessed Are the Peacemakers

We spoke for no more than 15 seconds...probably about 15 years ago now. Yet, I still remember what she said to me that day.

It was a Sunday morning, at the door of the church, where most conversations are limited to...

"Good morning." "How are you." "Good to see you." "Come again."

She paused longer than most that morning and in response to something that I had said in the sermon that morning said to me, *"Everyone is a peace lover, but few people are peacemakers."*

She was the first woman to be mayor of the city in which we lived. I know now, in ways I did not know then, that the politics of running a town or a city or a school is never easy. One is always faced with a never-ending progression of competing demands each the most important and the most urgent. I am sure that being the first woman mayor made the situation even that much more complex.

Maybe it was because of who she was. Maybe it was because of the respect with which so many in the city held her. But mostly, I think, it was because of the deep truth of her words that they have stayed with me for so long.

"Everyone is a peace lover..."

Desiring a sense of security and peace in our homes, in our communities, in our schools, in our world.

Wishing everyone would just be nice or at least be civil.

Wishing that bullies would not throw their weight around on playgrounds...or in offices or in politics.

Wishing that differences could be resolved without winners and losers; without hitting or killing. Wishing that we didn't have to worry about handguns and bombs or sticks and stones.

It is also easy to want to avoid conflict.

It is easier to go about our work or go to school or out into the community pretending that the bullies aren't there or telling ourselves that there is nothing that you can do about them anyway or to pretend that the demeaning or prejudicial comments that you hear don't really mean anything or don't really hurt.

It is easier, in the face of the complexity and the confusion and the conflict, to pull back and to draw smaller and smaller circles around our lives. Circles over which we, at least, have some control. To build the walls and to install the gates...either physically or legally or emotionally. It is easier to care some, but not care too much.

It is easier to turn away.

It is easier to be safe than sorry.

I know all that. I feel all that deep within me.

My natural tendency is to avoid conflict.

And when I can't and I stand in that uncertain mix of emotion and anger and confusion, my stomach churns and I lay awake in bed at night. When I find myself in places like that, I have to will myself to stay at the table and to stay in my seat or stay with the conversation because my natural tendency is to want to jump up and to run away.

"Everyone loves peace," she said, "but few are peacemakers."

As we continue to think about *"those things that make for peace"* this Advent, maybe it is important to think for a moment about what *peace* is and what *peace* is not if we are going to take the Bible seriously and consider what it means to be a peacemaker and not just those who think that peace is a good idea. Peace is not a lack of conflict, but it is a commitment not to resort to violence – either physical or emotional or spiritual. Peace is not everything remaining as it is, but it involves a deepening commitment to a complex reality of liberty and justice for all, and a willingness to do what it takes to help move from where we are to where we believe God would have us be. Peace is not just silence and calm, but also includes the passionate exchange of ideas and opinions that may, if we allow it, lead us to better, more equitable solutions and outcomes. Peace is not the absence of struggle, but the presence of love.

Peace involves the deepest possible respect for the other.

Peace demands the highest personal and corporate ethic that we can imagine.

Peace calls us to love our neighbor – who sometimes appears to us to be our enemy... to love the other as we would love ourselves.

Peace asks everything of us. And sometimes costs everything.

That is why, I think, there are so few peacemakers.

So here we stand a week away from Christmas. These days that are a poignant reminder of the dream of God that strikes a deep and responsive chord within us and shakes awake a hope lodged in our soul. A dream and a hope that often we can barely know or name, but that we sense is there. God would not be so cruel as to allow us to dream dreams that were not also possible.

The truth is.
God's dream then and God's dream today is possible.
Not only that, but it is entrusted to human hands and hearts.
Mary and Joseph's then...
Yours and mine today.
And, we are left to decide.
"Everyone is a peace lover, but few people are peacemakers."

While I believe that God can do what God chooses to do and that God sometimes acts in ways beyond our insight and understanding, I also believe that God waits for you and me.

97

It was the Jewish scholar Hillel who first wrote the words I sometimes use in worship, *"If not us, who? If not now, when?"*

It is St. Teresa of Avila, the Christian mystic, who wrote:
Christ has no body now on earth but yours; No hands but yours;
No feet but yours; Yours are the eyes
Through which is to look out Christ's compassion to the world; Yours are the feet
With which he is to go about Doing good;
Yours are the hands
With which he is to bless now.
"Blessed are the peacemakers for they shall be called the children of God." Jesus said.

You? Me? Can we dare to not just love the idea of peace, but to learn what it means to make peace? Can we dare to pray the prayer and then to follow the prayer with the daily decisions and actions of our lives?

You remember the prayer. You said it a few moments ago.

Lord, make me an instrument of your peace!
Where there is hatred, let me sow love;
Where there is injury, pardon;
Where there is doubt, faith;
Where there is despair, hope;
Where there is darkness, light;
And where there is sadness, joy.
O Divine Master, grant that I may not so much seek
To be consoled as to console;
To be understood as to understand;
To be loved as to love;
For it is in giving that we receive;
It is in pardoning that we are pardoned;
And it is in dying that we are born to Eternal Life.

May it be so.
For our sakes.
For God's sake.
For the sake of the world in which we live...
Which in the end is the only world that we will ever have.

Seatbelts in Church

Sometimes I think that we have it all wrong.

All this stuff about God and church. About Jesus and love.

About goodness and grace and the strength to get by.

Sometimes I think that we have it all wrong.

I dress up. You dress up. Nice clothes. Pleasant smiles.

Cordial words across the room.

We sing our hymns and say our prayers to God.

Or, to a God mostly of our own making?

Sometimes I think that we have it all wrong...

I know that church pews are not the most comfortable places to sit for a while, but compared to some other places where we might sit, and where others do sit...

Dirt floors. Prison cells. Park benches. Hospital rooms.

Cushioned pews in a warm room, especially one as beautiful as this, is maybe not as bad as it might seem.

Sometimes I think that we have it all wrong.

Is Jesus really that kind and gentle?

Is God really that safe and secure?

Or, do we pretend in order to protect ourselves? Who we are and what we think and how we act? Repeating the words, but not really hearing them. Singing the hymns, but not really meaning it. Worshiping carefully, without risking too much?

With incredible insight and a skeptics honesty, in her book *Teaching A Stone to Talk*, Annie Dillard writes:

Why do people in churches seem like cheerful, brainless tourists on a packaged tour of the Absolute...On the whole, I do not find Christians, outside the catacombs, sufficiently sensible of conditions. Does anyone have the foggiest idea what sort of power we so blithely invoke? Or, as I suspect, does no one believe a word of it? The churches are children playing on the floor with the chemistry sets, mixing up batches of TNT to kill a Sunday morning. It is madness to wear ladies' straw hats and velvet hats to church; we should all be wearing crash helmets. Ushers should issue life preservers and signal flares; they should lash us to our pews. For the sleeping god may someday awake and take offense or the waking god may draw us out to where we can never return. (p. 40)

Sometimes I think that we have it all wrong.

This morning I find myself wondering about the God in the Bible.
The One whom we say we worship this day.
The One in whom we say we place our trust.
The God whom I find in the Bible is anything but safe and secure.
The God of the Bible is...
Jealous. Passionately loving. Fiercely loyal. Determined. Committed. Angry. Strong.

When encountering Jesus, the One whom we believe was filled with the presence and promise and power of God, the unclean spirits cry for their lives with a human voice that sounds too much like mine, "*What have you to do with us...with me? Have you come to destroy us...to destroy me?*" Does encountering God feel something like that? And Jacob lying down to sleep one night, wrestles all night long with an unknown assailant, sweating and lurching and holding on for dear life. Is this the God we desire to meet?

I suppose that we could write it all off as Biblical fiction or ancient imagination. But, to tell you the truth, I take the Bible more seriously than that.

While a literal understanding of the stories we read or, understanding each word as being historically accurate is <u>not</u> the way to read the Bible.

Neither is overlooking the truth nor discounting the insight these stories contain.

While we would like God, like life, to be safe and secure. Something that we can understand and control neither God, nor life are like that, I think.

The stories that the Bibles tells are true.

There are unclean spirits which haunt human lives. Demons that lurk in the shadows of your life and mine. Evil that walks abroad in the world.

Are there not?

At least there is in my life and world, if not in yours. Not little red devils with pitchfork and pointed tails. If that were all there were, we would get off easy. But the unclean spirits that play on my fears.

Fear I will be recognized for the fraud that I am.

Fear that all I strive so desperately for does not matter.

Fear that I will fail. Or succeed.

Fear that what I do or don't do, does, in fact, ultimately matter.

The unclean spirits that prey on our arrogance...

That we are better than those whom we see.

That we are justified for that which we do.

That we entitled because of who we are.

I don't know about you, but I have wrestled all night with demons or angels. I am not sure which.

But I hate such moments...

I would rather sleep peacefully than face the fear or wrestle with angels.

I hate the confrontations which stir up the calm I work so hard to maintain. I hate the confusion and I hate the struggle.

I hate the questions and I hate the uncertainty.

I hate the challenge and I hate the anger

But sometimes I think that I have it all wrong. For...

Could the life-giving God who cries out in pain giving birth to all that is...

Could the lifesaving God who gasps one last breath while tied to a cross...

Could the everywhere God, who blows through the staleness of your life and mine with the both gentleness of a breeze and as a gale force wind...

Somehow and somewhere wait to mix it up with us during it all?

Could it be that if I really mean what I say and want life and world to be different from today, that I must...

That we have...

To begin to take seriously the passionate and fiercely loyal love of God?

To begin to take seriously the power of Jesus?

To begin to take seriously the words of the Bible?

To allow God to be God, and not something we create, if we are to find the courage, we need to face the fears that the demons expose?

To contend with the unclean spirits who trouble our lives?

To wrestle with angels until the break of day.

Holding on for dear life until we secure a blessing for us and for all. Even if it means we walk away with a limp.

Sometimes I think that we have it all wrong. And that what we do here protects us from God.

And keeps us from coming face to face with the Holy. The terrible, wonderful, life changing, life disrupting Holy.

For it we took seriously that God could be here in this place in this moment right now…

We would hold on for our lives and demand seatbelts in church.

Too Close to Home

Like me, do you swallow hard when you hear this story from the Bible?
Like me, do you want...
To push the Bible away?
Or turn to another pager...?
To use this story as an example of how impractical Jesus and the Bible and organized religion really are?

While I am quick to look for other ways to understand this text, a part of me continues to think that on that day Jesus meant exactly what he said. Especially when I open the mail and read a letter from an investment firm which begins:

Dear Mr. Alcorn,

As a person of wealth...

And, I look up from my desk and see a picture, given to me by a friend, of a Salvadoran family standing in the doorway of the stone and mud house.

But, believing what I do, I cannot push the Bible too far away. So I continue to grapple with the text.

Is there something here in this story that hits too close to home and which causes me to swallow hard that waits for you and me to understand? Is there something here other than a stark...

Either/or?

Or Yes/no?

Or a sell all you have or turn away?

Something that you and I can begin to grapple with that might enable us to take, at least, a small step forward in our life and our faith.

Maybe the question behind the encounter, and behind the question the young man asked behind the response which Jesus gave...

Is this:

"Is being good enough?"

Sometimes *being good.*

Following the rules.

Obeying the commandments.

Is the best we can manage.

Especially in those moments when life pushes in seeming to squeeze the life right out of us. And, those moments when the demands outweigh the energy that we have. And, those moments when concerns and burdens weigh so heavily on our hearts and minds that they bend our backs and slow our steps.

In those moments we find ourselves only able to do the best that we can. *Being good*, in those moments, may be good enough.

Sometimes *being good* and following the rules and obeying the commandments is the best for which we can hope.

In a day with too many guns in the hands of too many people and some of them far too young.

In a day when movies market violence and lyrics use language that belittle the humanity of others.

In a day when values and morals and character are debated on a national stage.

In a day when we debate having to 10 commandments in courtrooms and in classrooms and on television talk shows.

It raises the question that if we, at least, followed these rules we might all be better off than we are right now. At least, it might be a place to start.

The young man, in the Gospel, comes to Jesus, conscientiously and thoughtfully, having done everything that he was supposed to have done. Much like what you and I try to do. He kept the commandments. He obeyed the law. He honored his parents. He observed the Sabbath and worshiped God. He had always been truthful.

But, it seems, from his question, like he sensed that there was something more. *"There is."* Jesus said.

It was easy to get this far in my thinking as I tried to think through scripture and sermon. But it was a friend's comment that came in the course of conversation as we talked about how we could design an experience that would help college students, many of whom drift away from the church, think more deeply about world and life and faith that provided a clue. An opportunity so that as they think about God and faith it is something more than what they learned in 4th grade or 6th grade or 8th grade. He used the word *vocation* to describe what he hoped college students might experience.

Vocation...

The Webster's dictionary that sits on my desk defines *vocation* as:

A summons or strong inclination to a particular course of action: a divine call to the religious life.

In the Roman Church, vocation is often understood to be the calling of priests and nuns and those who join religious orders. In our tradition it is what God calls each of us to do and be as we come to understand and to take our place in the community of faith. But I like Frederick Buechner's definition better. He defines *vocation* as:

"Where your deep gladness and the world's deep hunger meet."

Now my words, not his... Vocation is...

Where the best of you meets the very real needs out there.

Where the life-giving energy within you meets the life starved world out there. Where the God in you steps out to meet the God out there.

Whatever it is within you that is your source of strength and joy...

Whatever it is within you...

That fuels your creativity...

That provides your enthusiasm for living...

That inspires your best dreams...

That awakens your conviction and courage...

Whatever it is within you that sustains your depth of Spirit...

Whatever it is, Jesus tells us, it is not just for you and yours.

"Where your deep gladness and the world's deep hunger meet."

That is what Jesus said to that young man and the invitation that Jesus extended to him. That is what God asks of each of us.

That is what the world needs of us.

Sometimes being *good* is the best that we can do and the best that we can hope for.

But we need to remember that you and I are called to something more.

More Than A Three Letter Word

A Sermon for Graduation Sunday

Several years ago, I came across the results of research on the religious perceptions and preferences of high school students and young adults. (Search Institute, Minneapolis, MN) The study included several interesting and sometimes troubling findings for those of us in the "church" business. One was this: That the more education one has the less likely one is to be actively involved in organized religion." And so to those of you who are graduating...after Sunday School and Confirmation and High School Youth Group and work trips and with that finding in front of us, we send you off to college with our prayers wrapped around your lives to acquire additional education and, if the information in that study is correct, to risk never seeing you in a church again except maybe to get married or to attend a funeral.

Once I got over the initial impact of what the study was saying, I realized that the results were not surprising to me at all. I am ashamed to say it, but by and large, we, meaning the Church (with a capital "C") have, or will be about to, let you down. In a couple of months, you will head off to college, and to classes and to knowledge that will open up the world to you. You will learn things and study subjects that, right now, you can only begin to imagine. All the while, for the most part, your understanding of God will remain static...locked up in the imagination and the images of a teenager. And I know this...the understanding of God that you had when you met with me each Sunday night when you were in Ninth Grade and in Confirmation, will not match up to the way you will think about life and world a year from now or two years from now or twenty years from now.

Do you remember the quote I gave you in Confirmation on one of the first Sundays we met? From the book *Your God is Too Small* by J.B. Phillips:

No one is ever really at ease in facing what we call 'life' and 'death' without religious faith. The trouble with many people today is that they have not found a God big enough for modern needs. While their experience of life has grown in a score of directions and their mental horizons have been expanded to the point of bewilderment by world events and by scientific discoveries, their ideas of God have remained largely static. It is obviously impossible for an adult to worship the conception of God that exists in the mind of a child of Sunday School age, unless he [or she] is prepared to deny his [or her] own experience of life. If, by great will, he [or she] does do this, he [or she] will always be secretly afraid lest some new truth may expose the juvenility of his [or her] faith. And it will always be by such an effort that he [or she] either worships or serves a God who is really too small to command his [or her] adult loyalty and cooperation.

I don't want that to happen to you.

I believe too deeply in God and I believe too much in you to send you off to college without at least raising the question with you one more time.

So, with everything else you will learn and everything else you will experience and all the discussions and debates that will stir your passions and tease your intellect…

Remember that God is more than a three-letter word.

For me, that which I know and name as God has nothing to do with an old man with a beard who lives in heaven somewhere and has everything to do with mystery and awe and wonder and love and life and courage and vision. It has to do with the values that I chose to live by…seeking justice and loving kindness and treating others the way I would want to be treated. And, my understanding of God underlies my conviction that I am connected to and responsible for all those around me – not just my family and not just my friends, but also for those forgotten others. Those who the Bible would name…God would name…my faith would name…as my neighbors.

The truth is we each are invited to search for an understanding of God; a way of thinking and talking about who or what God is for us that matches the circumstance of life in which we find ourselves. A book that I am currently reading reminds us *"that there are many faces of God, and each of us sees a different profile."* (*The Search of Belief* by Joan Chittister, p.11).

Might that be true for you as well?

That you are to search for an understanding of God…a profile of God…that keeps pace with your understanding of the world?

And, as you head off to college also remember this…

And that not all religion is narrow minded, or out-of-touch with life and world, or judgmental. You come from a congregation which believes that literalism destroys. Literalism, in whatever form, demands more non-thinking than it does genuine faith. We believe and do our best to speak in a religious voice that is inclusive, not afraid of questions and smart.

So, now go with our blessing and surrounded by our prayers.

Never settle for a "too small God" because God is always more than a three-letter word. And, come back. To add your new insight to ours; your emerging questions to ours; your growing faith to ours.

P.S.

The quote/gift I gave to graduating high school students was a quote by the Rev. Fred Rogers, a Presbyterian minister and the creator of the pioneering children's television show *Mr. Roger's Neighborhood*. The Rev. Rogers wrote:

The purpose of life is to listen….to yourself, to your neighbor, to your world and to your God. And then when the time comes to act…Act in as helpful and creative a way as you can.

As God to Each Other

For all the preparation and attention it receives, Christmas ends abruptly. At least in the Bible.

Turning the pages and reading the story, for the most part the Gospels go immediately from birth to baptism. Not baptism in the loving arms of Mary mild, but baptism in the arms of John, who eventually (at least as the Bible tells it) gets himself killed for speaking truth to power. Luke, who surrounds the birth of Jesus with angels and shepherds and heavenly hosts, describes Jesus' baptism this way:

John said to the crowds that came out to be baptized by him, "You brood of vipers! Who warned you to flee from the wrath that is to come? Bear fruits worthy of repentance. Do not begin to say to yourselves, 'We have Abraham as our ancestor;' for I tell you, God is able from these stones to raise up children to Abraham. Even now the ax is lying at the root of the trees; every tree therefore that does not bear good fruit is cut down and thrown into the fire."

And the crowds asked him, "What then should we do?" In reply [John] said to them, "Whoever has two coats must share with anyone who has none; and who has food must do likewise." Even tax collectors came to be baptized, and they asked him, "Teacher, what should we do?" He said to them, "Collect no more than the amount prescribed for you." Soldiers also asked him, "And we, what should we do?" He said to them, "Do not extort money from anyone by threats or false accusations and be satisfied with your wages."

As the people were filled with expectation, and all were questioning in their hearts concerning John, whether he might be the Messiah, John answered all of them by saying,

"I baptize you with water; but one who is more powerful than I is coming; I am not worthy to untie the thong of his sandals. He will baptize you with the Holy Spirit and fire. His winnowing fork is in his hand, to clear his threshing floor and to gather the wheat into his granary; but the chaff he will burn with unquenchable fire."

So, with many other exhortations, he proclaimed the good news to the people. But Herod, the ruler, who had been rebuked by him because of Herodias, his brother's wife, and because of all the evil things that Herod had done, added to them all by shutting up John in prison.

Now when all the people were baptized, and when Jesus also had been baptized and was praying, the heaven was opened, and the Holy Spirit descended upon him in bodily form like a dove. And a voice came from heaven, "You are my Son, the Beloved; with you I am well pleased." (Luke 3: 7-22)

So, it was for Jesus…at least as Luke tells it.

But, where does that connect with your life and mine? Maybe here…

Once again, it was a conversation with kids, this time three teenage girls, whose playful insight caught my attention. I share this story with their permission.

On the Friday before Christmas, the Middle School Youth Group was getting ready for a Midnight Run. Fourteen or so middle school kids with enough energy to put a dent in the energy crisis, along with Linda and Vic Fried and a few other adults sorting clothes, making toiletry kits, preparing coffee and bag lunches to take into New York City to share with those who find themselves living on the streets.

I stopped in to say hello.

As I walked in three girls came up to me. Two of them I knew. The third they introduced to me. "This is Christina," they said. Our Mom is her Godmother."

A brief aside…

In the Presbyterian Church, we don't officially have Godparents, those who make promises to care for the child being baptized and to take responsibility for the child if something were to happen to the parents. Instead, each time we baptize someone, the whole congregation participates and makes a promise like the promise that a God-parent would make.

Do you, the people of this congregation, promise to openly share your faith with this child and through your fellowship to strengthen her ties with the household of God?

112

Now back to the story....

"This is Christina," they said. Our Mom is her Godmother. That makes us God-sisters or God-cousins or something like that."

God-sisters? God-cousins? I wonder?

How often is it that how we see ourselves or describe ourselves and the roles we take on determine what we do or how we act?

I am a father. I am a husband. I am a pastor.

I have been a soccer coach and a school board member.

You are a mother. A parent.

A banker. A business person. An artist.

A friend. A student.

Do you see where I am going?

These "frames of reference" that we place around our lives and use to describe ourselves, in some ways, determine how we respond and how we act.

Most of you, if not all of you have been here when we have celebrated a baptism. Most of you have been baptized yourself.

So, what if along with all those other ways that you think about who you are, what if you also began to think of yourself as...

A God-sister; A God-brother; A God-friend;

A God-neighbor; A God-co-worker; A God-whatever.

God's very real, very human, very tactile – standing next to them and with them and for them – presence to those around you. If you thought of yourself in that way...

Would it change how you saw yourself and viewed your life?

Would it change how you viewed others and your interactions with them? Would it change how you would act?

Someone once said (I don't remember who) "Your life may be the only Gospel another ever reads."

Now, back to Jesus for a moment…

As I read the Bible, it was not birth or angels or the arrival of the magi that was the defining moment for Jesus, but baptism.

And somehow, in that moment and from that moment on, he saw himself and lived his life as "God's son…the Beloved."

And he became to those who knew him…

And to those who know him…

A God-brother and a God friend and a God-teacher.

God's presence to those who came into his presence.

In some small way are we to do the same?

"That makes us God-sisters or God-cousins or something like that," they said to me. You are right. It does.

Bad Theology

The old quip is still true. *"If you don't stand for something, you will fall for anything."* And "falling for anything" happens all around us and to us each day.

Well meaning. Seeking to be faithful. Going to church on Sunday people. Just like you and me.

Falling for anything...and we hardly notice.

Not because we want to or mean to, but because in our day-in, day-out world we tend to think of ourselves as business people; as parents; as citizens and not as theologians.

Yes, theologians. Those who take seriously the "study of God".

Identifying and naming the values to be keep close to the center of your life.

Who have the words and the ways to say what you DO believe and not just react to or shake your head at what you don't believe.

And, because we forget we are to be theologians...

Business theologians. Parent theologians. Citizen theologians.

We don't make the distinction between good theology and bad theology.

And we don't recognize the bad theology for what it is and where it is and so run the risk of "falling for anything."

What prompted my thinking about this was the bad theology I recently read and heard. Not the bad theology of Pat Robertson or some other TV preacher, but the more insidious and more subtle bad theology pushed by Madison Avenue.

Two advertisements, in particular, caught my attention. The first was for a watch. The tag line in the advertisement read, "Wear your bonus on your wrist."

Given the way the stock market and the financial industry has been lately that ad may translate into a Timex, but you and I both know that was not the watch the ad was pushing. So, for a moment, at least this morning, be a theologian and think about the theological questions this advertisement raises.

Questions...

About who God is and what God intends.

About values.

About our relationship to the world in which we live.

I found myself thinking about two things.

First, I found myself wondering if that is how God would really have us use our money...for a watch that costs far more than what most of God's children must live on not just for a year, but maybe closer to a decade? Second, I found myself thinking about the young people from our congregation (and so many of you in different ways). Young people who, in a couple of weeks, will wear gloves, and not a watch around their wrists as they bend steel and mix cement to make another safe home for a family. In the world in which we live and for which we are responsible – light of the world/salt of the earth, if Jesus is to be believed – which matters more, I wonder? Which is more important? A watch or (symbolically) work gloves?

The second ad that caught my attention was for a luxury automobile. I forget the model, but it doesn't matter. The tag line for this commercial was, "You deserve the good life."

Again, the commercial raises theological questions, don't you think?

Questions like:

What do I deserve?

Does a $40,000 car or a $60,000 car somehow equal the "good life" meaning the more expensive the car I have the better the life I have?

What really is "the good life"? How would you define it?

The bad theology around us is insidious. Impacting not only our lives, but maybe even more so, the lives of our children.

So, the question for us this morning is this…

How do we become clear about what we stand for so that we don't fall for anything?

How do we become so explicit about what we believe and what we value that when we are faced with decisions and choices our "good theology" begins to balance out the "bad theology" that we are inundated with every day?

Just like you, I face those same pressures every day.

And, like many of you, our family faced those pressures as our children grew up.

Over and over again we found ourselves saying, "That is not what is important to our family." And, we would do our best to point out and to name the "bad theology" when we saw it and heard it. And we included our children in helping to make the choices between "the bonuses on our wrist" – whether toys or trips – and those causes or concerns or ways to spend our money that were important to them and to our family so they would begin to learn how to distinguish between the two.

But, back to TV for a moment and one commercial that came closer to getting it right. The ad was not, at all, referring to God, but the tagline was on the mark. It was a commercial for Foot Locker that ended with: "You are what you believe."

You are what you believe. So, what do you believe?

117

About that which we know and name as God?

About your and our responsibility in and for the world in which we live?

About the core values that you would have be the guide for your everyday living? About how we should treat others?

About our relationship to and the use of the resources – time, energy, money – that are at our disposal?

About what you deserve in the relationship to what others deserve or need? About what the "good life" really looks like?

These are not rhetorical questions posed by a Sunday morning preacher and meant to be left hanging in air. These are heart and soul questions about who you are and who you desire to be. About who we are and who we desire to be. The truth is we answer them one way or another each and every day.

So, I urge you to take seriously your role and responsibility as a theologian. As a... A business theologian.

A parent theologian. A citizen theologian.

And not leave the task to Rachel or Katherine or me.

Or leave it to one hour on an occasional Sunday morning.

Because if you don't know and can't say what you stand for out there, you run the risk of falling for anything.

And, after all, both Jesus and the Foot Locker ad just may be right: You are what you believe.

So, as a reminder, remember this:

You are the light of the world.

How God Sees the World

The world in which I grew up was very different from the world in which my children grew up. Maybe every parent says that, but even so it is true. I am not talking about...

- Typewriters vs. computers.
- Email vs. snail mail.
- Rotary phones vs. cell phones.

I am talking about the maps on the wall.

The world *looked* different to me.

The world looked like the pull-down map that hung in the front of every classroom I ever sat in as a child.

- Flat map.
- The United States LARGE in the center.
- The rest of the world arranged around it.

And, if I had been asked to imagine a map of the universe, I might have imagined a map that looked roughly the same. United States. World. Universe.

But my children grew up with a very different "picture" of the world. They grew up understanding that the world looked like this picture of the earth for space and not like the flat pull down maps of my childhood. What a fundamentally different starting point for their thinking about life and responsibility and community when the world like that is their primary image. Years ago, when I showed that picture to a group of children and asked them what they noticed, one little girl responded, "There are no lines." In moments like that how often it is that our children tell us the truth.

There are no lines.

No lines between United States and Mexico.

No lines between Sudan and Chad.

No lines between Israel and the Palestinian territory.

No lines between Russia and Georgia.

There are no lines. Look!

But, despite her wonderfully innocent insight, you and I are smart enough to know all about lines. Aren't we? The lines we know to exist even if we cannot see them. Not only the imaginary lines drawn deep in dirt or sand marking the boundary between us and them, but the lines that divide...

Liberal and conservative.

Citizen and immigrant.

Rich and poor.

Black and white.

Red from blue.

Make no mistake, we know all about those lines. And we watch as those lines are dug deeper and deeper each day.

And, at the same time, we watch as the walls built on top of those lines climb higher and higher each day. So high, in fact, that we often can no longer see over the top to even glimpse those who reside on the other side. The picture of our world that looks like this [earth from space] and the reality of our lives stand deeply at odds.

So, then the question is, at least for us here today as Christians and as People of Faith who do their best to turn their lives in the direction of God and what God intends, the question is not only how do we see the world, but how does God see the world? More like this [earth from space] or more like the reality we know with its lines and walls crisscrossing communities, country, lives and world?

More like this [picture of earth from space], I think.

And, if that is true how do we get from where we are closer to where and how we believe God intends it to be?

I am not smart enough to have an answer or arrogant enough to <u>think</u> I have the answer, but I do have a suggestion for where and how we might, at least, begin the conversation. This is not a political suggestion. It is not a partisan suggestion. It is probably not even a practical suggestion. But it is a Biblical suggestion.

And, for you and me gathered here, believing what we say we believe, maybe, it will give us a place to begin.

Do you remember the words from the heart of the Torah?
Hear, O Israel…
Hear, all you who believe in one God.
The Lord, your God, is Lord alone.

And centuries later when challenged to name the most important commandment, Jesus recited the verse he had learned as a child. From the heart of the Torah. And, possibly from the heart of God. *And you shall love the Lord your God with all your heart, all your soul and all your strength.*

What I am trying to say is this…

If we <u>really</u> believe in <u>one</u> God…

If we really believe that there is only <u>one</u> source of Life and Love…

If we really believe that there is only <u>one</u> connecting Presence linking us to each other and us to all and us to creation and that all that is bears the image of that One…

If we really believe that…

Then maybe we can begin there…

By paying better attention to what binds us together rather than quickly being trapped by what pulls us apart. This does not mean that we will not disagree, but maybe when we are tempted to dehumanize or mock or belittle each other or call each other names through clenched teeth,

121

we can step back long enough and refocus on that place where the Bible begins.

The Lord your God...
The Lord our God, is Lord alone.

If we could, at least, do that, maybe we – you and I as People of Faith – could start pushing that impossibly large stone up the hill as we begin to inch our way towards seeing the world and seeing each other the way God sees us – all of us.

A world more like this [earth from space]

Than our mental maps crisscrossed with lines and walls.

Live the Way You Pray

Lord, teach us to pray, they said.

Did they want to be sure that they had it right?

Right words. Right cadence.

For God to hear through the cacophony of other prayers

Flung up towards God.

And, do we say it, too?

Lord, teach us to pray.

For, do we, like them,

Want to be sure we get it right?

Right words. Right cadence.

To make sure God hears Our one small voice

So God knows and understands

What we, so much, want God to do.

But, the words do not matter much, I think.

Not nearly as much as our longing to pray;

Or the intimacy and immediacy we know and feel

When the force of our prayer

Cracks open our hearts;

And unsettles our spirits;

Making room in both;

For both God and each other.

Lord, teach us to pray, they said.

And, we say, too.

Yet, I think we know how for we pray each day.

Sometimes, yes, with whispered words.

Please. Thank you. Help me. Help them.

And sometimes without any words at all.

Prayers released.   Heaven-ward flung.

Upward. Outward.

With the touch of a hand. A knowing glance.

A caring word. A heart-wrenching gasp.

Our prayers matter, I think.

Not as some magical formula preordained from on high

Given by God so that God might hear.

But as that fundamental connection that links our lives.

My life to yours. And our lives to theirs.

And all lives to that Source of all Life.

For in that moment when we dare to pray

Placing our strength alongside another's need;

Wrapping our care around another's sorrow;

Using our hope to push back the darkness;

Allowing another's joy to find a partner with whom to dance.

In that moment we come close.

Dangerously close.

Life-givingly close.

To one another and to God.

Our prayers matter. That we pray matters.

But we are not to live by prayers alone as if our prayers were somehow enough.

For if we get up off our knees;

And open our eyes;

And remain where we are or where we have been;

Our prayers dry up like old autumn leaves.

Useless and brown. Broken to pieces under trampling feet.

Instead our prayers

While aimed towards God are sent back to us;

To be for our lives a God-given compass

Pointing us in the direction we are to go;

Showing us, once more, how we are to live;

Outward. Onward. Towards someone. To do something.

What?

God only knows.

But you know, too.

For they are your prayers.

Flung towards heaven.

Sent back to you.

Lord, teach us to pray, they said.

And we say, too.

Yet, do we know what we ask?

For, you are to live;

We are to live;

The prayers we dare this day to pray.

What I Learned About Faith While Trying to Learn to Dance

A couple of weeks ago, when Vaneese Thomas and James Williams were here to share their gifts of gospel music with us, I mentioned that I am not a very good dancer. The primary reason is I become too self-conscious when the music starts. I find myself feeling like the tin man from the *Wizard of Oz*. The other reason is that I have a hard time sensing the beat of the music. I remember asking Frank Di Minno how people knew when to clap along with the music. His response was, "You clap on 2 and 4." I didn't have the heart to ask him "How do I know the difference between 1 and 2, and between 3 and 4?" And then, to make matters worse, when I watch others dance, I fall prey to one of the seven deadly sins – envy.

So that brings me to a couple of weeks ago and to the Hoedown the Deacons organized for us. When it was time to get ready (we were to come dressed for the occasion), I pulled out my cowboy boots out of the closet, dusted them off, put them on and was ready to go. At least as ready as I was going to be. Fifty, or so, of us showed up around the corner at the Bedford Village Elementary School. We shared a potluck dinner in the school cafeteria and then it was time to dance. We started off with some square dancing.

"Good," I thought… Swing your partner. Do-si-do. Promenade.
I can do that."
Then it was time to learn a line dance.
The caller/instructor assured us it was simple.
All you had to do was count to 8.
"Watch," he said.
And, he demonstrated the steps several times for us to see. "Count to 8," I thought.
"I can do that."

So, we lined up.
Three or four lines across the gym.

I strategically took my place in the middle of the last line so that I could both watch the caller/instructor and all those other people who were brave enough to stand in one of the lines in front of me.

Count to 8.

I counted and watched and followed the people in front of me. I was doing it.

1,2,3,4,5,6,7…turn.

Now we were facing the side wall.

I could still watch others out of the corner of my eye.

"Count," I told myself.

1,2,3,4,5,6,7…turn.

Suddenly, I was in the "front" line.

There was no one to watch and maybe others were watching me.

"Count to 8. Count to 8." I told myself.

1,2,3…and I was lost.

When everyone else got to 8, after I became lost at 3 or 4, I could turn and watch again, and found myself being able to follow along. If this had only happened once, I could have chalked it up to learning, but it happened three or four times in a row. When I could watch others, I could do the dance. When I found myself in the "front" line and not able to see what others were doing, I lost my way.

But all of this is not about dancing is it?

It is about faith…and God…and how in the world you put into practice in your daily lives all the things that we talk about and learn about and remind each other about each week.

So, here is what I learned about faith while I was trying to learn to dance.

If we have someone to watch, we have a chance of learning and knowing what we are to do. And, maybe that is the most important reason that we come here each week. To watch and to learn from each other so we can learn the steps to the dance.

I know…

People tell me they can pray just as well on the golf course as they can in church. Others tell me they sense something of God as much when they are walking in the woods as when they walk into a place like this.

I know that. There have been holy moments in my life like that. Moments seemingly disconnected from all the trappings and rituals and politics of organized religion.

Standing outside on a cold winter night and watching my breath disappear into darkness of the night and the brightness of the stars.

Looking out our kitchen window at the grass which seems to have turned green overnight and the forsythia shines like the sun.

And, I resonate with what Sean Cunningham said last fall when he shared what he wrote about *This I Believe.* The miraculous was present in those moments when I have held my children.

Maybe for you it is art or music or dancing or walking that cracks open that "thin place" between your life and heaven.

I know all that...

But, while those moments connect me to that which is Holy, all too quickly...

The children fight or our 16-year olds act like teenagers rather than young adults or our children walk in the door and leave their stuff all over the house.

Or, I get cold standing outside.

Or, I look at my watch and it is time to go to work and the grass and the forsythia both disappear into the landscape.

Life intrudes on holy moments and we are back to trying to figure out what in the world it means...

To love our neighbor when our "neighbor" is the one whose actions or attitude we find either arrogant or demeaning or indifferent.

When we are left to figure out what it means to let "love justice and resist evil" when are trying to balance our check books or explain to our children why we think it is not a good idea right now to buy that toy or to make some sense of the headlines in the news.

When we are left to figure out how in the world we are to "pray constantly" when our teeth are clenched, and our stomach is in knots and we are to be in two places at once juggling multiple roles and responsibilities.

At least for me, it is in those moments that I most need someone to watch. 1, 2, 3, 4, 5, 6, 7, 8.

How about you?

So, with all of that…
These two questions:

Who do you watch so you know how to dance? And, can we help each other learn the steps?

Last week for the offering I shared with you that I learned something about giving by watching my parents put their envelope in the offering each week in the church in which I grew up. I learned something about taking children seriously by watching Mr. Procopio who was my 6th grade Sunday School teacher. I learned about prayer and a "grown up" faith from Rich Bell. I learned about what it means to be a pastor from John David Burton. And now, I learn what it means not to give up on the dream that the world can be a better place and that our lives can help make that dream come true from the youth and the young adults who I have the privilege to work with and to know. I "watch" all them and more as I try to figure out this thing called faith and what it means to live faithfully in the world as it is. Which brings me to this.

Who do you watch?

I had a conversation a week ago with Patty Warble, who is the Director of the Drug Abuse Prevention Council that for 15+ years has had office space in our church. Periodically, we talk about our work with youth and their families. Patty shared with me a statistic from a report that she had recently read that indicated that teenagers needed five additional adults, besides their parents, to whom they could turn for help or support. Five additional adults whom they could watch and from whom they could learn the "steps of the dance."

Maybe needing five other people doesn't stop when we turn 21. Can you name your five?

And, question number two...

Can we help each other?

Can this be a place...

Can we be a people...

That intentionally tries to help each other figure it out?

A place and a people who encourage and support each other; who ask the challenging questions; who don't settle for simplistic answers; who take God and all that God stands for seriously; and who believe that faith has more to do with the other 160+ hours each week out there, than the couple hours we might spend "in here?"

1,2,3,4,5,6,7,8

Can we help each other learn to dance?

Wherever You Are

Sometimes I like what Jesus has to say.

After all, there are enough times and enough places in the Bible when what he says stops me I in my tracks and makes me swallow hard. At least, that is, if I take him and what he says seriously. You remember some of those things he said, don't you?

His telling us…

To love our enemies.

To pray for those who persecute you.

That it is easier for a camel to pass through the eye of a needle than for a rich person to enter the Kingdom of Heaven.

To go and sell all that you have and give it to the poor.

That if you hand causes you to sin, cut it off. If you eye causes you to sin, pluck it out.

To take up your cross and follow me.

But maybe we have become so accustomed to the words that we really don't hear them anymore and because of that miss the radical nature of the Gospel. Or, maybe we are like the person who said to me one Sunday, "I quit listening when you read from the Bible and begin to listen again when you start to speak." Or, maybe we skim over what we don't like or don't understand only to stop and to focus on what we do like…

God is love.

You are forgiven. Go in peace.

Words we hang onto like a life preserver.

Like our lives depended on it.

And to tell you the truth, maybe they do.

But back the verse that I like:

"The Kingdom of God," Jesus says, "is among you."

The Kingdom of God!

Marcus Borg, who is the Hundere Distinguished Professor of Religion and Culture at Oregon State University, and the author of a number of books, including *Meeting Jesus Again for the First Time,* the best-selling book by a contemporary Jesus scholar and *The God We Never Knew,* named as one of "ten best books in religion for 1997, defines the Kingdom of God (that which Jesus says is "among us") in this way: "The Kingdom of God is the way life would be if God were in charge and Caesar was not."

So what might that look like?

If God were in charge no child would go to bed hungry tonight…or without a bedtime story and a kiss goodnight.

If God were in charge parents would not cry over children who are killed by bombers or by bombs…or by random acts of violence on their way home from school.

If God were in charge race would not matter and we would notice character before color and recognize all as bearing the image of God.

If God were in charge you would never find yourself walking alone through the Valley of the Shadow of Death (see Psalm 23). Instead, there would always be a hand to hold; an arm on which to lean; and someone walking alongside.

If God were in charge gratitude would stand at the center of our lives.

If God were in charge, we would pay more attention to waging peace than waging war. If God were in charge homes would be safe and safe havens for all.

If God were in charge, we would all would have enough and all would have a place. If God were in charge...

The Kingdom of God is...among you. Among you!

Not someday in the future when either God comes in apocalyptic furor or we finally get it right.

Not above you like some idea of heaven up there somewhere.

Not even within you making it yours alone.

But, right here and right now. Among us...just as we are.

Among you and the person on either side of you.

Among you and your children and your partner and your family.

Among you and your co-workers. Among you and your neighbors.

Among you and those whom you pass on the street or in the store or at school.

The Kingdom of God is among you...or has the possibility of being "among you" ...wherever it is you happen to be.

And so, if Jesus is right and this verse is true, then it tells us pretty clearly where we are to look for God.

Where we are to look for those signs and those moments...

Of grace and hope. Of forgiveness and community;

Of redemption and comfort. Of meaning and peace and strength.

Those Kingdom moments which hold something of God and God's dream for us and for all.

We are to look "among us."

Right in those places where we live and work.

In the midst of all the relationships that make up the fabric of your life.

So, maybe today we should take Jesus at his word that there is something about God and about what God desires for us and for all that is right here.
Or, could be right here and right now.
If we were to see it;
And, name it;
And, claim it;
And, live as if it were so.
Kingdom moments in our midst.
In that moment…
When we step away from selfishness and towards gratitude.
When we wrap our arms around those whom we love.
When we extend ourselves for the sake of another.
When our actions, in whatever way large or small, make the world safer and more hospitable and more hopeful.
When we stand with and walk with others in times of need.
When we do our best to make the circle around our lives as broad as the reach of God.

Allow me to digress for a moment to help make my point.

There is a wonderful story in the Bible found in Genesis 2 which is the old, old story of creation and of Adam and Eve. Basically, the story begins like this…

God has made Adam (Hebrew for *man*) and is now God is pictured as kneeling in the mud of the earth fashioning all the other creatures. When God finishes sculpting a creature, God then blows into its nostrils the "breath of life" and presents the creature to Adam who gives it a name.

As you read the story you realize that the creatures God makes do not begin "to be fully alive until Adam gives them a name.

The point I am trying to make is this:

When we call others by name;

When we name things for what they are they become "alive" for us. Real to us.

When we name moments of honest gratitude as a moment of God's Kingdom, it becomes that for us.

When look at another and, in their face, intentionally recognize the image of God, God Kingdom reigns in that moment.

When we take a stand for justice and peace — whether that is by refusing to denigrate another or naming an injustice or wrong for what it is when others want to turn away — we pull God's Kingdom into the present.

When we pray with and for one another...

When we call and take time to listen to how another is doing...

When we deliver a meal or send a card...

We should do so knowing and claiming the presence of God.

For naming those moments for what they are not only helps us to remember...

But it also helps to make it real. To make God's Kingdom real.

In their lives and in yours in that very moment.

"The Kingdom of God is among you," Jesus said.

Can you believe it?

Can you believe it enough to live it?

Whose Economy?

A Sermon for Stewardship Sunday

My grandparents,
My mother's parents,
lost everything in the Depression. Home. Savings. The money they
had generously lent to the person in business with my grandfather who,
one day, just disappeared - money and all.

My grandparents...
My father's parents...
Were more fortunate.
During the Depression my grandfather worked two days a week in one
of the steel mills outside of Pittsburgh, Pennsylvania. Two days a week
may not sound like much, but it was enough to enable them to keep
their home and to provide enough food for their family.

I am not an economist or a banker to see very far beneath the surface
of the last several months, but it is the specter of those days through
which my parents and grandparents lived that has been used to define
the turbulence of the financial crisis through which we now find
ourselves living. I don't know enough to know how close the analogy
comes to being true, but I do know that several weeks ago I wondered
if I should drop everything to go and to stand in line at the bank and
to ask for my money...wondering if it would be safer in a shoebox
under my bed than in a bank that I was not sure was going to be there
the next day.

These are uncertain times.
Troubling times.
Banks and business too large to fail have done just that.
Jobs have been lost. Other jobs teeter on the edge of uncertainty.
Home values decline.
Retirement plans shrink.
Financial indicators are awful (our children would use a different, more
graphic word.) You know the pressure, at least, as well as I do. Some
of you much more.

In no way do I want to minimize the reality of what has happened and is happening all around us – from Wall Street to Main Street; from brokerage houses to your house. But neither do I want to minimize what, each week, I tell you I believe. What I have stood in front of you on most Sunday mornings for nearly 20 years and said out loud about God; about gratitude; about who we are and who we are called to be; and about what we are called to do and what we are called to build.

Words that roll off our tongues much more easily when all is going well. And, words that stand up to be counted when things are not.

Words that when we hear them again, in moments like this…on Sundays like this…leave us to decide – really decide – how "true" they really are.

So, as you consider your life…
And the circumstances of the world in which we now live…
Consider also the gospel and this word for today from the Gospel of Mark:

When he went ashore, he saw a great crowd, and he had compassion on them, because they were like sheep without a shepherd. And he began to teach them many things. And when it grew late, his disciples came to him and said, "This is a desolate place, and the hour is now late. Send them away to go into the surrounding countryside and villages and buy themselves something to eat." But he answered them, "You give them something to eat." And they said to him, "Shall we go and buy two hundred denarii worth of bread and give it to them to eat?" And he said to them, "How many loaves do you have? Go and see." And when they had found out, they said, "Five, and two fish." Then he commanded them all to sit down in groups on the green grass. So they sat down in groups, by hundreds and by fifties. And taking the five loaves and the two fish he looked up to heaven and said a blessing and broke the loaves and gave them to the disciples to set before the people. And he divided the two fish among them all. And they all ate and were satisfied. And they took up twelve baskets full of broken pieces and of the fish. And those who ate the loaves were five thousand men. (Mark 6: 34-44)

Be careful how you listen to this story.

Because I do not think it is about a miracle that Jesus performs. Or even about a group of people suddenly becoming kind enough to share.

This story is told to answer this fundamental economic and theological question: Is there enough?

The disciples said, "No." Jesus said, "Yes."

The economy of the world claims that there is not enough. Never enough. So get what you can and hold onto it at all costs.

The economy of God claims there is enough for all.

And that is where you and I live – in that tension between these two economies.

But, if the only economy we look at or respond to is the economy "out there," I believe it will turn us inward and shrink-wrap our lives causing us to become and to live as fearful, smaller people. But, when we do our best to remember that there is another economy – God's economy – which despite outward appearances promises that there is and will be enough, then we have a chance of overcoming the fear which surrounds us and living as generous and grateful people facing in the direction of a generous and gracious God.

Which brings us to today and to Stewardship Sunday.

That Sunday when we ask members and friends of Bedford Presbyterian Church to consider their financial pledge to support the ministry and mission of our congregation for the coming year. And, to this question with which each of us will wrestle:

Is there enough?
Can there be enough?
Enough for you and for your family?
And also enough for the church and its ministry and mission and the countless ways it touches and transforms lives – yours and mine included.

I happen to believe that who we are and what we do is important every day.

I have had the genuine privilege of seeing and experiencing the impact that the witness that this congregation has had – that you have had – on the lives of others…both those who have grown up in our midst and those who live some distance from these doors.

But, maybe in these days, who we are and what we do is even more important…

Reaching out and doing what we can to help those around us who find themselves in need – both those in our own communities who face uncertain times, but also those who around us and among us who are the most vulnerable who may very well bear the brunt of this crisis. Helping our children learn something about generosity and our youth about their ability to make a positive difference in the world in which we live Refocusing our lives back towards the values we know to be important, but sometimes lose sight of. Being here…for that moment when you or your neighbor need a place to be.

Maybe more than ever…

In times like these…

Churches need to "stay open."

We need to "stay open" and to do those things which we do best, but which we can only do if we find some way to do it together. Each of us doing our part and those who are able digging a bit deeper.

These days, it really is the economy that matters. The question for us and for here and now is: Whose economy?

Lost in Your Own Backyard

Lost coin. Lost sheep.

"I once was lost, but now am found…"

I wonder…

When you hear those words, do you think they apply to you? Or, does it just apply to people like "them"?

Maybe like that group of "lost" people who gather in our church five times each week…fifty-two weeks a year. Most of them doing their absolute best "to be found." They come to find their way for one more day because they know, all too well, the cost and the consequences of "being lost." And each time they come they begin the same way.

"My name is xxxxxx and I am an alcoholic."

It is their honesty about who they are and where they have been. And their knowledge about where they are now and where they would like to be that is essential in helping them both to be "found" and to "find their way".

But this sermon is not about them.

But, about you and me.

About those of us who gather here one time each week, not five. Coming together for a hundred different reasons…

Because it is Sunday morning, and this is where you are on a Sunday morning;

Because you think it is important for your children;

For yourself as you seek meaning and purpose; direction and strength for your life. You come looking for hope.

And, after a long week "out there" you come to reconnect with the Holy; to come closer to that which pushes you towards your best self.

But do you also come because you know you are lost?

That somehow you know, with the honesty and the certainty with which they know. Those who gather on those other days in Fellowship Hall...

That...

Without God; Without each other;

Without some regular reminder of grace;

Without that time to refocus on what we know to be our deepest values and our bravest hopes;

Without that Holy push to expand our lives outwards towards that which God intends for us and for all;

That without all that...

You would surely be lost. More lost than you already are.

When you hear those words do you think they apply to you? I wonder.

And it may be our inability or unwillingness to do so deceives us. For the truth is I think we often are. Lost, that is.

One of the ways you and I get lost is in the crush of expectations that push in on every aspect and every moment of our lives.

Expectations...

To always appear successful;

To participate in the right activities and to belong to the right group or go to the right school; And, like the people of Lake Wobegon...to raise "above average" children.

And, I think we sometimes get lost amidst the busyness of our lives. So busy with work to be done and who needs to be where and what needs to happen next. So busy keeping track of it all and doing it all that what is sacrificed is time to nurture those relationships that stand at the very center of our lives; to build sustaining friendships; to carve out quality time for family; to allow for what the Bible names as Sabbath time – time intentionally set aside for mental and physical and spiritual renewal.

And, we get lost in our affluence.

An affluence which would trick us into believing that happiness is to be found in objects to be owned and which blinds us to the challenges and real-life needs experienced each day by a majority of God's children.

The reason we don't recognize ourselves as "being lost" is that it is so every day. We have come to accept it as "life as it is". Unlike the Israelites in the wilderness who knew they were seemingly lost in the desert. Or, the members of AA who know the cost of their abuse;

We are lost in our own backyards and most of the time we don't even know it. And, often, we recognize the cost only when it is too late.

So, what do we do?

Being lost at least some of the time myself, I don't have any easy answers to offer. Only clues that might point us in the right direction.

One clue comes from those in AA.

Change does not happen until we admit that we need to change. Admit that we are lost…or, at least, some part of us is lost.

Rather than just giving in to "life as it is or appears to be," we can admit that we long for something different. Something more life-giving and life-sustaining and begin making choices, both personally and professionally, in that direction. Yes, it will mean you give up something, but what will you get in return?

Another clue, I think, can be found in the gospels. In taking the chance to believe to be true the promise about that which is lost being found. That we are not just "out there" on our own with no choices or no options. That we can be found. That God wants us to be found. That God looks for us until we are found. That God desires for us, individually and collectively, meaning and purpose and direction and peace. That we can choose to turn around and begin to move in a new direction. That all this that we hear about God and what God intends for us and for all just might...just might...be true.

A final clue may be that which wisdom and tradition teach us about that which can help us turn our lives around and point us, again, in the direction of God. Attitudes and actions and ways of living like:
Gratitude.
Compassion.
Awe.
Wonder.
Sabbath.
Generosity.
Maybe we experience "being found" when we practice those things which turns us in the direction of the Dream of God.

So, what do you think?
Are you lost?
Do all those words apply to you?

Maybe we should start the service over and begin like this:
My name is Paul. I am lost.

There is More to Life Than Death

A Sermon for Easter

The women went to the tomb expecting to find death.

They knew what to look for because they knew what Death looked like
and what Death felt like. They stumbled their way to that God-awful,
God-empty moment bringing with them what little they had....
Their ointments and their oils.
Their broken hearts and their tear streaked faces.

In the face of Death, they came to do what they could.
They would say the "right words".
They would hold each other as they cried.
And then they would go home.
Heartbroken, but home.
Back...
To pay bills.
To cook meals.
To go back to work.
To raise children.
Heartbroken, but home.
Death having torn out another piece from their lives.

Going to the cemetery that morning they knew what to expect because
they knew what Death looked like and felt like.
Just like we do.

But "heartbroken, but home" is not how the story goes, is it?
The women, expecting to find Death, suddenly find themselves
standing face to face with Life and having no idea what to do. All their
oils and ointments and "right words" instantly became useless.

Expecting Death, they were heartbroken. Facing Life, they were afraid.
Are we the same?

So, what is this story in the Bible about anyway?

What is Easter about?

What is Resurrection about?

Is it about Jesus, and what happened to Jesus? Sort of.

But if we stop there, I think we miss the point.

If we stop there, making the story only about Jesus, we sanitize the story allowing it to be neat and clean brought out once a year like our good china and our special silver and our Easter bonnets to be carefully used and enjoyed and then safely put away again.

No, the story is not just about Jesus.

The story is also about the women and the disciples.

About their expectations and their surprise. About their fear that somehow becomes faith. About their disbelief that somehow becomes hope. About the haunting face of Death that somehow becomes the unexpected promise of Life.

And if I am right, and the story is more about the women and the disciples than it is about Jesus, then there is a chance... A *hold your breath and hope* chance that it is also about you and me.

And that's what we want, right? That's what we need?

A story with a surprise ending that is not just about then, but also about now. Not just about them, but also about you and me.

For you and I live in a world where Death is real. And where the minions of Death - hatred and violence and apathy and arrogance and despair - are real.

Every day real.

Get up in the morning and know it and see it and feel it real.

And we, like the women, have our own set of oils and ointments and "right words" to say that may blunt the pain, but they don't make Death go away.

But maybe…
Maybe today…
If we allow ourselves to be found somewhere in this story…
Allow it to be real enough and come close enough
And ourselves to be honest enough…
We might also find our way to the surprise ending.
And suddenly find ourselves knowing and find ourselves believing…
That there is more to Life than Death.

That there is more to Life than Death.

And is that not the surprising "stop you in your tracks" good news of Easter?

Jesus found that out.

The women found that out.

The disciples eventually found that out.

I don't know how it happened, but somehow in those days after Good Friday, with everything else in the world seeming to remain exactly the same – cross, Romans, heartbreak, fear – those who followed Jesus began to experience Jesus again with the only way to describe it as Jesus alive again. God real again. Only this time within them rather than just in him.

I don't know how Jesus became more real to them than "flesh and blood" real. But he did. I don't know for sure how that happens for you and me. I only know that it can, and it does. I think a part of it may that they let go enough to give God room. I think a part of it might be that they dared to begin to live how Jesus had lived with heart open and arms open and hands open looking for that elusive Kingdom that Jesus said is hidden in each and every moment. And, finding and holding onto and living the Dream of God into being somehow each day despite the uncertainty and the sorrows and the struggles that were and are and continue to be a part of life.

I wish I were wise enough to tell you exactly how to find your way from cautiousness to faith. From the Death that we know each day to the Life that God promises to us still.

The truth is that much of what I know is hearsay. Glimpses offered by others that seem to point the way.

Loving neighbor as self.

Swords into plowshares.

I have a dream.

Imagine.

Do all the good you can by all the means you can.

If you protect your life you will lose it. If you lose your life for the sake of another you will find it.

And while I can't draw a map, but only pass on some of what I have heard, I can tell you this. I have seen it sometimes. I have experienced at moments...

When love is most real.

When gratitude is most genuine.

When suddenly the fear and the selfishness that divides us disappears for an instant and I recognize you for who you are and who you are called to be.

I have seen it enough, but maybe even once is enough, to believe that what I have heard is true.

That Life is stronger than Death

That Hope is more powerful than Despair

That Resurrection is and will be the final word.

And having heard it and seen it we can chose to live it.

As the women eventually did.

As the disciples eventually did.

Living, each day, into the promise of the Resurrection.

Living, each day, the reality that there is more to Life than Death.

Subversive Imagination

Bonnie Gordon is good friend and on the staff of Bridges to Community. She lives in Masaya, Nicaragua and works in the communities surrounding Las Conchitas where a group from our church has worked each year for the past five years. Bonnie tells this story about her first trip to Nicaragua in the mid-1990's. The trip was one of the first for the new organization Bridges to Community. A small group of people went to the community of Tierra Colorada to help the community dig a well that would supply the community with fresh, clean drinking water for the very first time. If you were here a couple of weeks ago when Kathy Bruce and Liz Keeffe and Steve Skillman spoke of our recent trip to Nicaragua and saw some of the pictures from that trip, you can imagine how back-breaking and dirty the work of digging a well is.

One evening early in the week, Bonnie, who is never content to just dig wells or to build homes, came out of her tent with a large box of crayons that she had brought with her so that she could draw pictures with the children of the community. The result was magical and eye-opening all at the same time. The children had never seen crayons. Let alone so many colors neatly stacked in one box. Our children take crayons for granted. We throw them away when they break in half. These children carefully, reverently held and colored with each crayon. Daring only to ask for one color at a time.

When it was time to put the crayons away and to go to bed, one little boy asked if he could take three crayons home if he promised to bring them back the next day. Bonnie, of course, said, "yes." The little boy selected the colors he wanted and left. The next day he brought the crayons back and asked if he could take three more. It turns out he was taking them home to show his family because his family had never seen crayons before either.

Bonnie ends her story by saying, "In that moment my world was turned right side up."

Not upside down, but right side up.

Think about it.

It seems to me that here, towards the end of Lent, and as we approach Holy Week…

Palm Sunday. Maundy Thursday. Last Supper. Crucifixion.

Death. Burial. Resurrection. Easter.

That the question underneath it all is whether we look at life and world as being upside down or whether we are going to cast our lot with Jesus and give ourselves a chance of seeing and experiencing the world as right side up.

Here is what I think is God's invitation to us.
We are invited to see the world today as it might be.
As God imagines it to be.
As we pray for it to be.
As the best of our scriptures and tradition tells us it can be.
And, not just how it is.
God invites us to use a *subversive imagination* so that we not only see the world the way God sees the world, but we begin to live today like that world is possible. Which, if the Gospels are to be believed, is how Jesus lived.

I probably don't need to tell you, but here is a description of our upside-down world.

It is a world where there is never enough so we have to get all we can.

It is a world where strangers are to be feared and where differences lead to divisions. It is a world of scarcity and want.

It is a world where power translates into "power over."

It is a world where death is stronger than life.

It is a world of the "survival of the fittest" and we better make sure we are the "fittest."

It is the world of this morning's headlines in the New York Times and The Washington Post and La Prensa and on Al Jazeera.

It is the world in which you and I live each day.

But God...
And Jesus...
And, the best of the Bible...
Tell us of something very different.
It tells us of a way of living...

Where there is the promise of enough for all;

Where strangers and outsiders are named as neighbors.

Where we are to treat others as we would like to be treated.

Where giving and taking are not antonyms, but synonyms.

It is a world, where in the poetic imagery of the Bible...

Bread is given in the wilderness (see the story of the Exodus).

Where children are given in the eleventh hour (see the story of Abraham and Sarah).

Where exiles are given a home (read the Jewish prophets).

Where the blind see and the lame walk and the oppressed are given freedom.

Where the dead are given new life (listen to words and life of Jesus).

And we are left to decide which way the world really is. Upside down or right side up.

Now, before you accuse me of too much naiveté, I want to tell you that I do know the reality of the world as it appears to be.

I know the pressures of raising children.

I know the work that it takes to sustain relationships over time.

I know the struggle to make difficult choices in that grey area between right and wrong. I know something of the political reality of dealing with power and differing agendas in the world.

I, like you, know the reality of the headlines in the news.

But, even with all that, the question remains the same.
Upside down or right side up?

We can just give into it all and say to ourselves "That is just the way the world is." Or, we can take our prayer seriously when we say, "Thy Kingdom come." And, if we chose the latter rather than the former, here is how Jesus/The Bible tells us we are to live...

We are to be a light to others that not only dispels darkness, but also ignorance, prejudice, hatred and bitterness.

We are to seek reconciliation whenever and wherever possible. We are to keep the commitments we make.

We are to say what we mean and mean what we say.

We are to love our enemies and to pray for those who seem to stand against us. We are to know what is most important and what is not.

We are to put God first.

We are to measure ourselves the way we measure others. We are to treat others the way we want to be treated.

We are to live believing in abundance rather than scarcity.

We are to live grateful lives and from our gratitude learn generosity.

Somehow. Someway. In our day in, day out living...
We are to do our best to live our lives in the direction of God...
Allowing God's subversive imagination that was embodied in Jesus...
To turn our lives, and maybe even some small piece of our world...
Right side up.

And, every once in a while...

Every once in a while...

Something as simple as crayons...

Or a home or a smile...

Will prove to us beyond a doubt that we are facing in the right direction; And that moment will bring God's Kingdom close;

And, will help us to find our lives before we lose them.

I Need A Hero

I have a confession to make.

When I am driving around in our car, I am a sports radio junkie.

I feel a little bit guilty because a part of me thinks that I should be listening to NPR or some other station or show that is more interesting or more thought provoking or more intellectually stimulating. And sometimes I do, but then I find that I can't help myself. I push the next button and return to a sports station to find out who won and why or who lost and why. As I was listening one day, I discovered that one of the sports radio stations has a time when listeners can call in and "rant" about anything they want for 30 seconds. I share this with you because I want to "rant" this morning. To share with you something that has been getting "under my skin" for some time now.

Because I write each week for worship and preaching and because I do my best to use language in a way that is thoughtful and meaningful and evocative, I notice how language is used by other people and used in the culture around us. I also have a sense of the impact of language on how people think and act. For example, I think we numb ourselves to the reality and devastation of war when we refer to sports events as "battles" and civilian casualties as "collateral damage". Does using language like that make sports more important than they should be and war more like a "sporting event"? And, I think we cheapen serious social and political debate when the language used in the public arena demeans or demonizes those who take different positions than we do. There are countless examples of that on both the radio and the TV each day. But, before I get to far afield from what I really want to say, here is my 30 second "rant":

With all due respect to those who serve in our Armed Forces; who risk life and face an overwhelming task, particularly in Iraq and Afghanistan; a task that I cannot begin to imagine… And, with all due respect to police officers and firefighters who give so much each and every day to protect our lives and our communities, I am tired that they are the only ones that are ever held up in front of us as "heroes". Individuals lifted up to a level that we would want to emulate; that we would want our children to emulate. They may well be, but they are not the only ones.

I don't' know about you, but I need…
And I think our children need…
And I think our communities need…
And I think our country needs…
And I think our world needs…
A different kind of hero to look up to and to follow.
End of "rant".

So, on this Sunday…
When we baptize a child and wrap our dreams around a tiny life. And recognize those young people in our congregation who are graduating from high school. And remember and celebrate so many other transitions that take place at this time of year in the lives of those who grow up in our midst who we have pledged, time and again, to care for and to support, I want to think about "heroes" and the type of heroes I think we need.

I need a hero…one that is mature enough to be wise about the ways of the world, young enough not forget their idealism and their dreams and bold enough to challenge my complacency and cautiousness.

I need a hero…one that is willing to show us how to connect our best skills and talents to our bravest hopes and our deepest values; who is willing to live amidst the complexity of the world with their minds in sync with their souls.

I need a hero…one that not only thinks about a career, but considers, also, a vocation: that place where the best of them and the world's deep hunger meets.

I need a hero…one that will work as hard for peace as our armed forces work in waging war.

I need a hero…one who is a steady presence; who, in the midst of all that happens, models respect and hard work; and who teaches us, by example, what it means to be grateful and kind and considerate amidst all the circumstances of life.

I need a hero…a mother and a father who work as hard at being parents and community members as they do at being successful.

I need a hero…one who will stand up and look around to see what is needed or what is lacking in their communities, especially what is needed among those who have the smallest voice and the least access to resources and then do the hard work to alleviate that need, even if it takes years.

I need a hero…

We need heroes…

Like this.

The truth is, I think, It is not that we don't have them.

It is that we don't name them for who they really are.

I am reminded of the first verse of the 12th chapter of the Book of Hebrews in the New Testament which reads: *"Since we are surrounded by so great a cloud of witness…"*

Thankfully we are… Thankfully I am…

Surrounded, that is, by witness upon witness; hero upon hero.

They build homes.

They volunteer in our schools.

They visit senior citizens who are homebound.

They stand and talk on a street corner in Manhattan at 1:00 in the morning with the man who will sleep in the cardboard box.

They drive neighbors to the doctors.

They teach a second language to hard working parents. They hand out an extra bag of groceries.

They read to their children. You get the idea.

The list is endless.

You can name them just as I can. These, too, I think are heroes.

Everyday people...as heroes always are.

In their own way shaping and changing the world...our world...God's world entrusted to us...for the better.

These are the people I want to grow up to be like.

These are the people I want my children to grow up to be like.

I want us to know them...

And name them...

For who they really are.

And to hold them up as a model for others to follow.

The quote I gave to our graduating high school students is this: *"We are the ones we have been waiting for."*

When we are tempted to wonder why something is not being done... We are the ones we have been waiting for.

When we find ourselves complaining about the lack of leadership...? We are the ones we have been waiting for.

When we long for more peace and less violence in the world in which we live... We are the ones we have been waiting for.

When we wonder why so many are hungry... We are the ones we have been waiting for.

When we wonder why no one is willing to speak up or do "what is right" ...

We are the ones we have been waiting for.

When we look around and say to ourselves that we...

Or our country…

Or our world…

Needs a new kind of hero.

Remember this…

We are the ones we have been waiting for.

A Sermon in Verse for Christmas

In the beginning
The very beginning
The first word spoken by the Great God Almighty
In that instant before creation exploded into being
Rushing headlong to takes is place
In that great expanse and mystery, we call space

The first word spoke by the Great God Almighty was Immanuel.
God with us and God within us.
God with sunlight and starlight
God with moonbeams and mountains.
God with Father Adam and Mother Eve.
God with.
And God with Eventually Jesus.
Imagined by God
Dreamed into being by God
From that the very beginning From that very first instant
When creation rushed headlong to takes its place.

Jesus
Who somehow heard the reverberations of that very first Word
That echoed still
Bouncing off the ends of space and human hearts
Jesus who heard that Word
And began singing it
And saying it
And living it
Until he became It
So much so that
When others looked at him they saw something of God
When they listened to him they heard something of God
When they walked with him they found themselves walking with God.

But the world waits now as it waited then
Not in solemn stillness waits

But with the rumblings of war
And, the groans of the weary
And, sometimes drowned out by the songs of the pious
Waiting now as it has always waited
For someone else to hear that Word
That reverberates still
Waiting for someone else to sing the song.
For someone else to allow
Some small part of that first Word of creation
To penetrate their heart
And to prick their conscience
And to find someplace within them
Deep within them

So deep within them that it begins to take over.
So each breath taken recaptures a wisp of that very first breath that
spun stars in their courses
So each word carries with it an echo of that very first Word
So each act becomes an act of dreaming into being the great Dream of
God.
Takes over them like it took over Jesus
Like it has taken over others
Turning life upside down and inside out
Until they see
And you see
And I see
Creation as it was imagined in that very first instant
And not how it is today.

And in that moment when the very first Word of the Great God
Almighty breaks
Through our façade
And through our resistance
Incarnation happens again
And again
And, thank God, again.
And in the end is this not really what it is all about…
All our carols
All our candlelight

All our comings and goings
That this first Word of God spoken first from the very beginning

Is not past tense, but present tense
Not was, but is
Not then, but now
Not him, but you.
And is that not our biggest challenge
And our most promising hope?

In the beginning
The very beginning
The first word spoken by the Great God Almighty
In that instant before creation exploded into being
Rushing headlong to takes is place
In that great expanse and mystery we call space
The first word spoke by the Great God Almighty
Was
Is
Immanuel.

Reflections

Grey Clouds

So what about today?

The day I have

The moment I have

Right now

But never again?

I pace.

Impatient with the chill in the air

And the low hanging clouds.

Closing me in.

Weighing me down.

Wrapping landscape and life

In their greyness.

I pace. Impatient with myself.

The trees outside my window wait.

Or ready themselves at a depth

And with a silence

I cannot see

And am not yet wise enough to understand.

Reminding me

I still have so much to learn.

Walmart

I needed a haircut.
And, our dog needed new food and water bowls.
But, after nearly 30 years of the same routine.
Same barber.
Familiar stores.
Knowing, roughly, how long it would take to get from here to there
Having now moved, finding everything "new" takes some time and searching.

So, after driving by a couple hair salons relatively close to where we live which advertised haircuts for both men and women but looking in the windows and only seeing women getting their hair done, I tracked down a barber shop which was about 30 minutes away and open when I needed it to be. Before I left home, I made my list of other things we needed while I was out, including new dog food bowls. I typed the address of the barber shop into my phone and was on my way. I found the barber shop, parked in the parking lot across the street and went in to get my haircut. It was just the type of barber shop I had been looking for.

After getting my haircut, I walked back to the car ready to find my way to the next stop on my list. Dog food bowls.

When I had arrived, I was focused only on finding the barber shop and so had not paid much attention to anything else. Now that I had accomplished that without getting lost, I was able to notice where I was and what was around me.

And, there, in front of me, was a Walmart.
I don't usually shop at Walmart.
But it was there. And, convenient.
And, if they had dog food bowls, it would save me an extra stop on the way home.

Two things struck me as I went into and walked through the store.
The first, was the very visible reminder that not everyone has the financial resources to shop at Target or Macy's or you name the store

you most often shop at. The second was the three staff members with whom I interacted as I found my way to the pet section caught me off guard as they smiled at me, asked how they could help (and did help) and, when our interaction was over and I had said *Thank you*, looked me in the eye and said they were glad they could.

Two takeaways from my 15 minutes in that Walmart.

First, based on my interaction with those three employees, I would shop there again just because of how I was treated. Graciousness and simple kindness made a difference. (I know every employee is probably not like the three with whom I interacted, and I have other, larger ethical concerns about Walmart, but I was treated better at that Walmart than I have been treated at many other stores at which I have shopped.) Second, despite my "knowing" it and wanting and working on it to be different, I was reminded again of how quickly and how easy I/we project images and expectations on those whom we perceived to be different. Lesson learned…again. I walked out of the store not only with my dog bowls, but as a better person.

Anyway Haircut. Check.

Dog food bowls. Check.

Two more stops then on my way home.

Reminders

We went to church again last Sunday.
It was nice.
The people around us were welcoming.
The pastor was honest and thoughtful with what she said.
In a variety of different ways, we were reminded of the communities
around us. From those down the street to those across the world.

But, what I left with was this.
For one hour
Out of the 168 hours in my week I was reminded of goodness.
And, compassion.
And, gratitude.
And, grace.
Those words were said out loud.
Both to me and for me.
And, more than that, I said those words out loud.
To me and for me.
And also, to and for you.

I was reminded of the larger circles around my life.
And, that we are made for each other.
And, are to care for each other.
And, that I am not (and neither are you) the center of that circle.

I was also reminded I was not perfect.
(Something I already know all too well.)
But in the next breath,
I was reminded that, even though I am far from perfect, I am valued.
And valuable.
And, have the ability and the opportunity
In the moment before me
To make myself better.
And the world around me better.

All of that in one hour.
Only one hour.

Out of the 168 hours in my week.

In the other 167 hours of my week
Between the news
And the social media posts
And the grocery store checkout lines I am reminded how petty we can be.
And, how thoughtless and uncaring we can be.
And, how inhuman we, too often, are.
For 167 hours each week we are bombarded by the reminders of our worst selves.

But for that one hour....
We dare not forget the horror and the heartbreak with which so many people live.
But we should not forget the goodness either.
In ourselves.
And, in each other.
I, for one, need the reminder.

Were You Raised That Way?

Were you raised that way?
Did your father teach you…
To disrespect women?
To laugh at someone who has a disability?
To go around calling other people names?
To always blame someone else?
Were you raised…
To believe lies?
To mock others?
To snicker when another person stumbles?

Did your mother teach you…
To clap your approval over someone else's embarrassment?
To treat another person in a way you would never want your children
to be treated?
Or your partner to be treated?
Or, yourself for that matter?
Or, did you learn it on your own?
Or, do you act that way to go along with the crowd?

Do you feel ashamed
As I did as a little boy
When I did something wrong on the far side of town, but my Mom
found out what I had done
And how I had acted
And how I had treated another person
And was waiting on the porch for me when I got home.

If how you just acted
How you just treated that person
Especially one who is different from you in some way
Is the last memory we have of you…
Is that how you want us to remember you?

Men We Have a Problem

Politics aside…
Women are abused and harassed at an alarming rate.
On a daily basis.
BY MEN.
Men like you and me.
Men like the ones we know and work with.
Men who go to church or temple or mosque with us.
Men who we see at the Post Office or the grocery store.

Women bear the brunt of the problem, but let's be clear.
They are not the problem.
We are.
Too much history.
Too much bad theology.
Too deeply embedded cultural norms.
Make it easy to push what happens/what we do aside with some excuse. After all *boys will be boys*.
Or, they were just *sowing their wild oats*. Or, *she asked for it*.
All of that is WRONG.
And, we have to be the ones who stand up and say it is wrong.
Not Christine Blasey Ford.
Not Chris Wallace's daughters.
Not the women who confronted Senator Jeff Flake in the elevator.
Not all the women who called the local and national abuse hotlines following the Senate hearing on Thursday to report abuse. Many calling and speaking out for the very first time.

Here are some statistics from the National Sexual Violence Resource Center:
- 1 in 5 women and 1 in 71 men have been raped
- 1 in 3 women and 1 in 6 men have experience sexual violence

And, from a report by NPR…
81% of women have experienced sexual harassment.

A friend and colleague wrote this yesterday on his Facebook page. I share it with his permission. *One thing that ought not get lost in the he said she said of Judge Kavanaugh's hearing is that regardless of the outcome of this case there continues to be an ongoing tragedy in our culture. Women are assaulted, demeaned, raped and disrespected all the time. That is the truth no matter the facts of this case. Dr. Ford spoke the truth and it is an ugly truth very much alive in our world. This must be addressed no matter how much the power structure wants to avoid it. Shame on us for this where so many women relate to her tragedy and too many men act like it just doesn't exist.*

And, this which a friend shared on her Facebook page.

We talk about how many women were raped last year, not about how many men raped women. We talked about how many girls in a school district were harassed last year, not about how many boys harassed girls. We talk about how many teenage girls got pregnant last year, rather than how many boys and men impregnated teenage girls. So you can see how the use of the passive voice has a political effect. It shifts the focus of men and boys and onto girls and women. Even the term "violence against women" is problematic. It's a passive construction; there is no active agent in the sentence. It's a bad thing that happens to women, but when you look at the term "violence against women," nobody is doing it to them. It just happens to them. Men aren't even a part of it.

Men we have a problem.

Ordinary Day

I don't have much to write about today.

This morning I got up and took a walk

For half an hour along a dirt road

While the air was still cool and the sun was warm.

When I got home, I took our dog for a walk.

Letting her off the leash and watching her run across the field.

I went to the store and bought a new belt and a new pair of socks.

I came home and had lunch.

Leftovers.

And talked with my wife while we ate.

Nothing special.

Very ordinary.

Everything special.

Nothing ordinary.

The Opposite of Love

Today's quote from Sojourners:

There are two basic motivating forces love and fear.
When we are afraid, we pull back from life.
When we are in love, we open to all that life has to offer with passion, excitement,
and acceptance. — John Lennon

Is that true?

That the opposite of love is not hate, but fear?

Fear of what comes next.

Fear of those who are different. Fear of what we do not know. Fear of losing what we do know.

If that is so, would that change how we respond to others?

Instead of working to overcome hate, we would seek to alleviate fear.

What questions would we ask?

What attitude would we adopt?

What would we do different than what we are doing now?

Just asking.

And, wondering....

Letting Go

It is Tuesday.

A work day.

I am here at my desk because that is where I am supposed to be on a Tuesday. Where I have been on Tuesdays for most of my adult life.

But today is different.

For the most part, my office is empty.

There are more books in boxes than on my bookshelves. Several pictures remain on my desk.

They will be the last things I pack.

I remember a story I read some time ago about a parent going for a walk with their child. As they walked, they came along a stone wall. And, just as my children did when they were young, the child wanted to climb up and walk along the wall. Once up on the wall, the parent reached out to take the hand of the child. Only this time was different. This time the child pushed the hand away and declared, *"I can do it myself."* Of course, she could. Of course, he could. And, with confidence and courage the child walked down the wall while the parent, no longer needed in the same way, watched.

Today, I feel a bit like that.

Not the child part, but about the letting go.

What I have had a hand in or on for so long is no longer mine to hold.

I let go.

And watch.

And celebrate.

And dream.

And pray.

These are people and this is a community I care deeply about.

More than I can put words around.

I have done my best to care for them and about them.

And they have cared for me.

As I said to them on Sunday…

I am who I am because of who they are and have been.

The gratitude runs deep.

Super Heroes

Each Sunday, during our morning worship, we invite the children who are present to join us on the front steps of the sanctuary for what we call our *Time with The Children*. This week it is my turn. I am not smart enough to know how ideas pop into my head, but as I wrote my welcome and my prayer for Sunday morning, I suddenly had the idea that for our *Time with The Children* I would become a superhero.

The nursery school in our building provided me with a red cape. The Children's Librarian at the local library told me she would find a mask for me. To top it all off, I made a cardboard shield. And, to prove I was a *real* superhero my shield has *Super Hero* written on it and lightning bolts. Of course, the children are going to tell me I am not a *real* superhero. That to be a *real* superhero I need some type of superpower like flying or super strength or swinging from building to building.

Then, I am going to ask them this.

If I was hungry and you shared your sandwich with me would I think you were a kind of superhero? Or, if I was new to your school and didn't know anyone and you sat with me at lunch and talked with me, would I think you were a type of superhero? Or, if it was winter and I was cold because I did not have a coat and you helped me find a coat which would keep me warm, would I think you were a type of superhero?

All of this reminds me of a story.

For more than 20 years I have been leading service learning trips to Nicaragua. On most of those trips we help with the construction of a cement block house complete with tile floor and metal roof. At the end of one trip, standing in front of his new house, the father of the family for whom we had built the house said, *"I have always dreamed of being able to provide my family with a home that had a floor and a roof. Thank you for my mansion."*

A mansion?

A 16'x16' home for his family of 5.

A space smaller than some of our bedrooms.

Maybe I don't need my cape and shield after all.

Say a prayer with me:

Dear God, help me be a superhero for good. Amen.

The Real World

Are you old enough to remember the early days of personal computers and the acronym *wysiwyg* which stood for *what you see is what you get* and meant what you saw on your monitor would match the finished document when it was printed. I wonder if *wysiwyg* applies to more than old computer operating systems.

What does the *real world* look like to you?
Survival of the fittest?
Might makes right?
A giant conspiracy theory?
The version of the Golden Rule which says, "The one with the gold rules?"
Does the real world look like today's headlines in the news?

I am not naive.
I know the world often looks like that and feels like that.
But...
What if the real world actually looks something like this?
More cooperation than competition?
More kindness and compassion than greed and violence?
More goodness than hatred?
More treating others the way they and we would like to be treated?
More beauty than ugliness?
More hope?
More peace?
More equality?
More justice?

What if that is the real world?
The world out there?
That world waiting for us to see it and name it and live in it.?
WYSIWYG

Maundy Thursday

When you remember me, it means you carry something of who I am with you. That I have left some mark of who I am on who you are. (Frederick Buechner) Believing that to be true, that Jesus has left some mark on each of us and all of us, this evening we remember who he was and what he did and the mark he has left on our lives.

Why is it that sometimes the most straightforward and the easiest to understand becomes the most complicated?

What did Jesus do?
He healed.
The paralytic.
The man possessed by spirits.
The woman who was bleeding.
Blind Bartimaeus.
Zacchaeus.

What did he do?
He fed those who were hungry.
The 5000.
The disciples on the shore and on their way to Emmaus.
Those who were searching.
The woman at the well.
Nathaniel who asked if anything good can come out of Nazareth.

What did he do?
He extended a welcome to the excluded and the disenfranchised.
The women who interrupted Simon's dinner party to wash his feet.
And the woman who pushed her way through the crowds to just touch his robe.
The children who the disciples tried to keep away.
Those who were sick or blind or deaf.
And, he included the stranger.
The Samaritan.
The Canaanite woman.
The Roman officer whose son was dying.

What did he do?
He challenged those who misused authority and power.
The religious elite.
The Roman overlords.
Those who acted in his name, but who then used that authority for
their own ends.
He made the circle which encompassed God's children larger.
As a colleague said,
Moving the margins until there are no more margins.
That is what Jesus was about.

What did he do?
He healed.
He fed.
He welcomed.
He included.

And those of us who follow Jesus, are left with this question.
Is our call to stand on the sidelines and watch?
Or, are those of us who have heard his voice and who dare this night
to eat the bread he offers and to share the cup he blesses and who day
in and day out say we follow in his footsteps to do what we have seen
him do?

Which World?

This past weekend I officiated at a wedding.
The groom is from the United States.
The bride is from Ecuador.
So far. So good.
Then this.
The father of the groom is Sri Lankan.
The mother of the groom is Danish.
The guests at the wedding represented seventeen nationalities or cultures.
Canada.
Colombia.
Uruguay.
Venezuela.
Mexico.
Uganda.
Zambia.
France.
The Ivory Coast.
Germany.
Denmark.
Palestine.
Syria.
India.
Sri Lanka.
United States.
Ecuador.

In addition to those seventeen, guests travelled from Egypt, Pakistan and the Democratic Republic of Congo to be at the wedding.

The world under one tent.
To celebrate two people, from very different parts of the world, who met, fell in love, decided to get married and to step towards the future together.

When I was growing up Catholics didn't marry Protestants.
Irish Catholics were discouraged from marrying Italian Catholics.
Jews did not marry Christians.
Christians didn't marry Muslims.

Blacks didn't marry whites.
Whites didn't marry blacks.
And, someone from the United States didn't marry someone from Ecuador.

Two very different snapshots of the world. Which world do you prefer?

I Hope

I visited my Mom this week. Her life is winding down.

I sat by the side of her bed and we talked. Small talk about the weather. Remembering trips we took as a family. Asking if she would like a sip of water.

In the silence between the conversations her gaze would be someplace else, and I would look at her wondering where she was and what she was thinking. When I interrupted the silence and asked, her eyes would refocus on me and she would seem surprised by the question. "I was just looking at the blankets stacked on the chair." She said.

While I will never know I hope, in those moments, she is someplace else.

Someplace beyond her hospital style bed.

Someplace beyond the walls of the skilled nursing facility which is now her home.

I hope she is someplace surrounded by the memories of my Dad.

And, the love they shared.

And, the years they had together.

And, their standing together to meet the challenges and joy of raising three sons and going to college and receiving degrees and fashioning careers and providing for their family.

I hope she is surrounded by memories of her children and grandchildren and her great-grandson. I hope their voices and laughter and presence fill her heart.

I hope she is lost in the love which surrounds her.

If Today Were A Day

If today were a day

To lay on your back

And look at the stars

Or the clouds

What would you wish for?

Hope for?

Dream about?

Got it?

Go do that.

Better Than You

Do I have to be?

Better than you?

Stronger than you?

Smarter than you?

More admired than you?

Liked by more people than you?

Do I have to be better than you for me to be me?

If I am not better does that mean I am less?

I wonder…

Is it really about winners and losers.

About winning at all costs?

About winning despite the cost? To you.

To us. To them. To me.

More and more

That way of thinking and acting

And being

Feels broken to me.

And destructive. With the cost and the damage

More than we can bear.

And, maybe more than we can fix.

Christmas Eve: A Benediction

What if God was a verb and not a noun.

More action than being.

And what if the same were true about Christmas.

Then maybe instead of:

Happy Holidays

Or Merry Christmas.

This.

Be peace.

Be hope.

Be light.

Be God with us.

Be Christmas.

My Prayer for You this Christmas

May there be room in your life for wonder.

And for mystery.

And for awe.

And for love.

May you catch a glimpse of God in the face of a stranger.

In the words of another may you hear the whisper of an angel.

Beyond the taxation of daily demands and expectations,

May you know and feel the call of God.

May there be time to hold the moment that is right now reverently and deeply.

May you lift your head to see the stars in the sky knowing one is there to guide you.

May you have the courage to offer the gift of your life in the service of Peace on Earth.

Too Small

But you, O Bethlehem, who are one of the little clans of Judah, From you shall come forth for me one who is to rule Israel, Whose origin is from of old, from ancient days. Micah 5:2

The Sufi Muslim poet, Rumi said:

You are not a drop in the ocean. You are the entire ocean in a drop.

Which makes me wonder...

When was the last time you felt you were only one person? Too small to make a difference? When was the last time you felt too insignificant to impact or to influence the change which, when you look around you and into your heart of hearts, you know needs to be made? When was the last time you felt too small to change the world? The last time you felt like a drop in the bucket to say nothing of a drop in the ocean?

Which brings us to today. And, to Advent.

And, to its miraculous, jaw-dropping story of the birth of Jesus. Not miraculous because of Mary or angels or wondrous star or wisemen who find their way. Miraculous because everything one would normally expect in a story like this gets turned upside down.

The holy city Jerusalem is replaced by backwater Bethlehem. Herod and his royal court are replaced by Joseph and Mary.

The Roman legions patrolling the countryside and streets in an effort to maintain law and order is replaced by the heavenly hosts who sing *Glory to God in the highest and on earth peace.* The Emperor Caesar Augustus is replaced by Jesus of Nazareth.

The drop in the bucket becomes the bucket. The drop in the ocean becomes the ocean. And, if this story is true, then this also is true.

The small things matter and can make a difference.

The kind word.

The caring touch.

The welcome extended.

And, this is true.

The forgotten shall be the ones who step forward and claim their place.

The disparaged shall be the ones whose presence helps to bend the long arc of history in the direction of the Kingdom of God.

The marginalized and the silenced shall be the ones who find their voice and sing and shout. And, this also is true.

Too small is no longer an excuse to do nothing.

Too insignificant is no longer a reason to turn away.

For if God can use Bethlehem God can use you.

If God can use Mary and Joseph God can use you.

If God can speak to the shepherds huddled in the field God can speak to you.

If wisemen can see and follow a star so can you.

Because you are the ocean.

Saints

As well as the demons which have haunted my life there have been saints. Not the kind you see in pictures. Or in the iconography in churches. But, the kind who sit next to you on the subway. Or, who coach your children's soccer team. Or, who volunteer at the local food bank.

Saints who are ordinary people.
Who, day-in and day-out
Do what they can and do their part
To make our communities and world better.
Closer to what God intends for us and for all.
Who do what they do because it is the right thing to do.
Their faithful response to the gospel which guides them.

It is saints like this who have picked me up and propped me up.
Who have cast out the demons which have haunted me.
Who have seen in me that which I could not see in myself.
Who have identified gifts.
And nurtured gifts.
And challenged me to dream bigger dreams than I dared to dream.

All of them have names.
Some I remember.
Others have been forgotten.
Many went unnoticed.
But all continue to surround my life as that great cloud of witnesses.

Today, for all the saints...
To all the saints...
Thank you for saving my life.

Resistance

When the mighty belittle the vulnerable

And the strong look down on the weak

Kindness becomes an act of resistance

And compassion an act of rebellion.

When fear and vitriol rule the day

And religion is wielded like a hammer

A smile becomes a sign of hope

And an extended hand an act of courage.

When words are used to divide and destroy

And taunts used to exclude and to blame

Integrity and truth become an act of defiance.

And a vision of the beloved community an insurrection.

Today All I Can Do Is Pray

Today, all I can do is pray.

There is no fixing.

No making better.

At the moment, even no helping.

And so, I spend the day remembering.

Doing my best to recall moments frozen now in time.

When I was…

When he was…

But those remembered moments make up only a handful of all the moments which reside somewhere within who I am.

I scramble to remember more.

Lost in the looking until I stop

And allow my *Thank you* to be enough.

I believe love reaches out beyond time and space.

And, prayers do the same.

Defying the laws of physics.

Holding us together even when we are not in the same room.

Today, all I can do is pray.

Advent

A day or so ago, a daily reading I subscribe to ended with this:

We have to say yes before anything, don't we?

The risk of that *yes*

Opens the door to that which comes next.

A *next* which is impossible to fully see or imagine until the word is spoken.

Advent is a season which invites and waits for our *yes*.

A *yes* to mystery.

A *yes* to gratitude.

A *yes* to possibility.

A *yes* to that dream of a better tomorrow.

A *yes* to the other.

Before any of this could happen.

Mary risked *yes*.

As did Joseph.

Now.

What about you?

What about me?

One Wish

What would I wish for you today

If I had a magic wand;

Or a wish to make upon a star;

Or one final wish to be made at my command?

What would I wish just for you?

Maybe this.

I would wish for you a vision;

A dream big enough and bold enough and brave enough

To match both your spirit

And the wonder and the complexity of the world as it is.

I would wish for room in your life for wonder and mystery.

I would wish for room in your life for beauty and grace.

I would wish for you to find your way

Through the sorrow and disappointment,

Which is sure to come,

To the life which awaits you on the other side.

I would wish for you a sense of gratitude,

Deep and ever deepening gratitude,

Which opens you up to the promise of life.

If I had a wand to wave or a wish to make

This would be my wish for you.

Santa Claus Is White

It is hard to believe, but the craziness around Christmas just got crazier.

A couple days ago, Megyn Kelly, a commentator for Fox News declared that Santa Claus is white. Her comments set off a rapid response from serious to comedic. But, if I take a step back from the craziness of it all, her comments made me stop and think. Apart from the debate about the history of Santa Claus, what does it mean if Santa is always white?

To tell you the truth, until this craziness erupted, I never thought about it. I never thought about what that meant to me. And, even more unsettling for me, I never thought about what it might mean to a person of color. Or, a child of color.

What does it mean if the great gift giver;
The person who knows if you have been naughty or nice;
Is a person you can NEVER look like or be?
Does it matter?
Until now, it never occurred to me to even ask the question.
And that is the unsettling part.
At some fundamental level I think it does matter.
At least for me.

Because in the largely white, largely Caucasian culture in which I live I need to remember that the world is much larger and much more diverse than the *white* world in which I live. Maybe it is me who needs to begin to imagine a black Santa or an Asian Santa or a Hispanic Santa as another small step towards seeing and understanding and appreciating the world as it really is. As God intends it to be.

A Walk in the Woods

I went for a walk in the woods today.

Up the path

Alongside the stream

Which rushed its way downhill

Until it found a deep pool

In which to rest for a while

Before going on.

There was no need to speak.

The steam said all that needed to be said.

And silence filled the woods around me

And my soul, as well.

Any words of mine would have been out of place.

An intrusion.

Upsetting the delicate balance between silence and stream.

I went for a walk in the woods today.

And, for a moment, at least, I was where

I needed to be.

Prayers

Eyes Wide Open

Even if we pray with our eyes closed, O God, Help us to live with our eyes wide open. Being caught off guard, again, by…

The incredible beauty;

The unquenchable hope;

The deep goodness;

The amazing grace;

Which surrounds us each and every day.

But also to see and to not turn away from…

The deep pain.

And, the very real hatred and fear.

And the faces of those who struggle all day, every day just to survive.

And, somewhere in that incredible swirl of names and faces, may we see ourselves, O God. Standing there amidst those who find themselves in need of hope and sustenance and forgiveness and grace and standing shoulder to shoulder with those who work each day to make their families and our communities and our world a safer, more equitable, less scary place for us and for all. For all those whose names we know and whose faces we see and whose needs we acknowledge our prayers this day.

May our prayers fly outward into the world You continue to love so much, O God. And, then, may our lives follow where our prayers first lead.

Amen.

All I See Right Now

Today, O God

I ask for a rainbow.

Or something.

Some small sign that goodness will prevail.

And decency.

And compassion.

And kindness.

Some sign that the flood waters

And the chaos

Are not permanent.

That the harm we are doing

To each other

And to ourselves

Does not have

Will not have

The final word.

I ask for a rainbow, O God

Because all I see right now

Feel right now

Are the waves

Crashing around

And into

The leaky boat which is my life.

Our lives.

Prayer for the Sunday of Memorial Day Weekend

On this Sunday of Memorial Day Weekend...
Let us pray for any and for all who have lost their lives in any conflict.
Their names remembered on bronze plaques and marked by crosses or stars or crescents that line far too many fields.
Let us pray for all the mothers who have lost a son.
And fathers who have lost a daughter.
And brothers who have lost a sister.
And children who have lost a parent.
And, let us pray for our country.
Our leaders.
Our fellow countrymen and women.
Those who are doing well and those who are not.
And, let us give thanks for freedom.
The freedom to go where we please.
To worship as we please.
To have a voice in deciding those who will govern.
And to express our own point of view.
And let us pray for ourselves.

For if we take God at God's word and claim our place among the People of God we are called to something more. And even though we can't quite see it, we are to live, work, speak, dream our way towards that day which may almost be *now*...

When the lion lies down with the lamb.
When swords will be transformed into plows.
And spears into tools to harvest food enough for all.
And when we will be named as peacemakers and because of that be known as the children of God.
For, if not us, O God, then who?
And if not now, O God, then when?
Amen.

Teach Us to Pray

Teach us to pray, O God.

With our words and with our hands.

With our hopes and dreams and with our lives.

With our heartbreak and our sorrow and with our kindness and our compassion. Teach us to pray.

Teach us to pray

That we might care for each other

And care for the stranger in our midst

And the overlooked among us

And the communities in which we live

And the world entrusted to our care and keeping.

Teach us to pray, O God

That our heartbreak over high school shootings

And those who have to stand in a line to see a doctor

And children who are afraid to go to school because they might come home and their parents will not be there

And those whose lives are torn apart by terrorists and bombs and hatred and racism...

Teach us to pray that we might offer more than just "thoughts and prayers."

Teach us to pray, O God.

When We Call

It is not as if you come only when we call, O God.
You are, in fact, present in each moment we have.
And, in all the moments we have.
As intimate and as close as the next breath we take.

It is more that we pause long enough to be reminded
And, to remind ourselves
Of Your abiding presence.
So, may this moment be one of those moments, O God.
When we stop long enough to allow our hope and our sorrow;
Our joy and our fear;
Ourselves and each other;
To be held, for a moment, in a deep awareness of Your presence.

We pray for all that has been entrusted to our care and keeping.
For those whom we love and those who we know.
For those with power and those without.
For those who are broken and those who rise up in hope.
For those who struggle for their daily bread and those who wage peace.
And for all those others we would name in this moment.
Into your hands, O God.

And, as always O God, may our lives follow where our prayers first
lead. Amen.

Call Us Out

Call us out, O God.
Call us out from all those places where we hide
From you and from each other.
Call us out from behind the walls we build.
And, from the stereotypes to which we cling.
And, from the assumptions and easy certainty which avoids the challenging questions which face us.

Call us out, O God.
To life.
To hope.
To justice.
To compassion.
In other words, O God, call us out towards your promised Kingdom meant for us and for all.

As we turn towards You, may we find the courage to pray.
For all those who we remember in this moment.
And, for all those who find themselves in need of health or healing or hope or a reminder of your abiding presence in all the moments of life.

And, added to all those prayers, O God, our prayers of gratitude for the love which surrounds us and for the love which supports us. For the opportunities before us and the responsibilities entrusted to us. Thank you for this community of faith with its reminder of who we are and whose we are and who we are called to be.
And, as always, O God,
May our lives follow where our prayers first lead.
Amen.

This Moment

In this moment which is now, O God,

But never again

Create some space within us we pray.

Push past our busyness.

And our lists.

And our focus on what comes next

Rather than the moment we have Right here.

Right now.

Stop us long enough that we might take stock of ourselves.

Who we are.

How we are.

Our dreams and hopes.

Our brokenness and sorrow.

And, to make room for the other and to leave space for you.

Those whom we love.

Those whom we barely know.

For all fall within the circle of Your love.

So, here we are, O God.

Create some space within us, we pray.

Amen.

Open Our Eyes

Open our eyes, O God, that we might see.

Both the world as it is and how it might be.

Open our eyes that we might see.

Both those whose lives are rich and full and those who struggle to find their way each and every day.

Open our eyes, O God, that we might see might each other and see ourselves and see that we belong to each and are responsible for and to each other.

Open our eyes, O God, that we might see we all belong to You.

May our prayers each day and our prayers today remind us of this.

Amen.

How We Pray

The truth is, O God, using words is usually the last way we pray. And, even then, our words barely scratch the surface.

Our hopes and dreams;

Our tears;

Our heartbreak;

Our compassion;

Our concern;

Go farther and reach deeper than what our words can ever go.

So just as we do every day, let us pray with all that and more.

Let us pray with our bravest hopes.

And, with the tears we cannot hold back.

And, with the brokenness of our heart.

And, with our compassion which reaches out a hand to our neighbor.

And, with our concern for so many in so many places;

Including this Your world entrusted now to our care and keeping.

Amen.

Learning from Lazarus

Call us out, O God.

From all those places where we hide from you and from each other.

Call us out from behind the walls be build

And, from the stereotypes to which we cling

And, from the assumptions and easy certainty

Which avoids the challenging questions which we face.

Call us out, O God.

To life.

To hope.

Towards your promised Kingdom meant for us and for all.

And, as we turn towards You, we can dare to pray.

For all those who have been named in our midst this day.

And, for all those who find themselves in need of health or healing or hope or a reminder of your abiding presence in all the moments of life.

Lord, hear our prayer.

And, added to all those prayers, O God, our prayers of gratitude for the love which surrounds us and for the love which supports us. For the opportunities before us and the responsibilities entrusted to us. For this community of faith with its reminder of who we are and whose we are and who we are called to be.

Lord, hear our prayers.

And, as always, O God,

May our lives follow where our prayers first lead.

Amen.

Invocation

Last night I had the privilege of offering the Invocation at Antioch Baptist Church's 39th Annual Martin Luther King, Jr. Banquet. The theme was *Honoring the Past, Shaping the Future.* Here is my Invocation:

We are a people used to praying.

Aren't we?

Praying in church.

Praying before a meal.

Praying when we get up in the morning and before we go to bed each night.

But today...

This evening...

Our praying needs to be more.

Maybe it has always needed to be more and has been more.

But today it feels different.

These are unsettled days and unsettling times.

So, as we remember the work and legacy of Martin Luther King, Jr. and honor the past, let us pray like this so we can continue to bend that long arc of history in the direction of God's Kingdom come and shape a future which we will be proud to hand to our children and grandchildren.

So today.

Tonight.

Let us pray not just with our words, but also with our hands.

Let us pray not just with what we say, but also with what we do.

Let us pray not just with what we intend, but with the witness of our lives.

Let us pray not just with what we dream, but also with our feet on the pavement.

Let us pray, not to implore God who already holds out before us that grand dream of God's Kingdom come but let us pray to remind ourselves and to remind each other of who we are and whose we are and, especially, who we are called to be.

Let us pray not saying *"Lord hear our prayer" but* pray so we might become agents of God's prayer echoing and embodying the witness of the angels who so recently proclaimed *"Peace on Earth. God's good will to all."*

We are already blessed, so I don't need to ask for that again

For either this gathering or for our food.

 Instead, this.

Thank you, God, for this gathering.

For the witness and work of these people.

For the strength and hope and courage in this room.

May we be strength and hope and courage for others.

Amen.

Remind Us, O God

Remind us of strength, O God.

The strength to care.

The strength to share.

The strength we can lean on

When we find life hard or challenging or painful.

Remind us of grace, O God.

A grace which heals.

A grace which opens us to hope.

A grace which meets us in the midst of each day

And turns our lives in new directions.

Remind us of Your dream, O God.

A dream of swords into plowshares.

A dream of a table large enough for all.

A dream of a time and a place where all are named and welcomed

As sisters and brothers.

And recognized as children of God.

Remind us of gratitude, O God.

For love which sustains.

For food enough.

For who we are called to be.

Remind us, O God, that *Thank you* is our first and our best prayer.

Remind us, O God.

Again.

Sometimes We Make It Too Complicated

Sometimes we make praying and prayers too complicated, don't we, O God. Thinking we have to be in the right place or say the right words in order to pray. But it is not like that, is it?

Remind us again, O God…

That each time our heart reaches out to another is a prayer.

Every thank you felt and said is a prayer.

Each time we listen carefully and caringly to another is a prayer.

Every time we gaze at another with love overflowing is a prayer.

Each time we reach out our hands to help another, it is a prayer.

Every time our heart breaks for another it is a prayer.

Each time we are stopped in our tracks by beauty is a prayer.

Every time we look closely at a flower;

Or gaze into the depths of space, is a prayer.

The lesson for us is to turn those moments into a lifetime.

Amen.

Today, O God

Today, O God

May our world be small enough:

And our imagination large enough;

That we might see beyond the horizon of what is;

And catch a glimpse of what is to be;

As we do our best to follow in the footsteps of Jesus. Amen.

Five Prayers for Today

One

I used to pray that God would feed the hungry, or do this or that, but now I pray that [God] will guide me to do whatever I'm supposed to do, what I can do. I used to pray for answers, but now I'm praying for strength. I used to believe that pray changes things, but now I know that prayer changes us, and we change things.

— *Mother Teresa*

Believing all fall within the circle of your love and care, O God, we pray.

First, for those who find themselves in need.

Those who are lost.

Those who are separated from their children.

Those without a home or a place to call home.

Those who are hungry.

Those who are victims.

And, we pray for those who have enough.

And more than enough.

Ourselves included.

May our affluence not lead to arrogance.

Instead, may gratitude deepen our compassion.

And, may we live with an awareness of our need for each other.

And, may we find our way forward towards that promised day when all will have enough, and all will have a place.

And, as we pray may our lives be changed.

So that we begin to pray not just with our words.

But also, with our lives.

Amen.

Two

Meet us where we are, O God, and just as we are.

Strong and fragile.

Whole and broken.

Hopeful and sad.

Meet us as we are;

Doing our best to find our way;

Trying our best to live with open minds and open hearts and open hands;

Turning our eyes and our lives in the direction of Your Kingdom come.

Meet us where we are, O God.

Right here. Right now.

And, then call us to more, O God.

Your more.

Let our prayers also reach out into the world

Entrusted now to our care and keeping.

Let our prayers reach out to all who find themselves in need.

The hungry.

The displaced.

The forgotten.

The victims.

And let our prayers encircle all who sing and dance for joy.

Our children.

Those who breathe in deeply the promise of today.

Those who do their best to love long and well.

And, as always, O God…

May our lives follow where our prayers first lead.

Three

In this moment, O God, we ask to be reminded.

Reminded that all fall within the circle of your care and concern.

Reminded that all are to fall within the circle of our care and concern.

Reminded, too, that we are to see not only what is,

But, also, what might be.

Remind us that we are to be agents and angels…

Of peace.

And of hope.

Of reconciliation.

And of compassion.

Doing what we can…

What we are called to do…

To bring that distant day close.

And so we pray…

Not just upward, but more importantly outward…

Wrapping our prayers around those whom we know and have named;

And, around all that has been entrusted to our care and keeping and so many more which we would remember and name in this moment.

And added to all that this, too, O God.

May our lives follow where our prayers first lead.

Amen.

Four

Open our eyes, O God.

And our minds;

And our hearts;

And our hands;

And our spirits;

So that in these everyday moments that add up to a lifetime we can see and recognize and name Your presence with us and among us.

Open us up, even just a crack, so we can see and name...

Your love and compassion and care and forgiveness;

Interwoven in the stories of our own lives;

Turning us;

Leading us;

Guiding us;

In the direction You would have us go.

Shaping us into the people You would have us be.

People doing their best to love the world and everyone in it the way You love the world and everyone in it.

And so, our prayers stretch out from our lives

Large enough and bold enough

To encircle and to embrace those whom we have named and more.

And, as always, O God

We pray that our lives follow where our prayers first lead. Amen.

Five

God, meet us where we are, but leave us not there.

Call us, again, towards Your Grand Dream meant for us and for all.

Be that light which draws us on.

Be that voice which speaks truth to us in the night.

Be that work of challenge or hope which stirs our spirits.

Be that presence which sustains our walking.

We ask it as we seek to follow in the footsteps of Jesus.

Amen.

About Paul Alcorn

For nearly 30 years Paul served as Pastor of Bedford Presbyterian Church in Bedford, NY a congregation known, among other things, for its commitment to the community and its service learning trips to Appalachia and Central America for high school students. Alongside his responsibilities as Pastor, Paul was instrumental in starting the Emergency Shelter Partnership, a program which provides a safe place to sleep during the winter for those who would otherwise be sleeping outside, the Westchester Youth Alliance, an interfaith program for high school students and the Rewarding Potential Scholarship, a program which provides significant financial support to help local high school students achieve their dream of attending college. His undergraduate degree is from The College of Wooster, Wooster, OH and his Master of Divinity and Doctor of Ministry degrees are from McCormick Theological Seminary in Chicago, IL. He is recently retired and living in Vermont. He continues to write on his blog at *We Get There by Walking* which can be found at paulalcorn.com.

CPSIA information can be obtained
at www.ICGtesting.com
Printed in the USA
BVHW041028190419
546008BV00017B/900/P